One-Block Wonders, encore!

New Shapes, Multiple Fabrics, Out-of-this-World Quilts

MAXINE ROSENTHAL & JOY PELZMANN

C&T PUBLISHING

Text copyright © 2008 by Maxine Rosenthal and Joy Pelzmann

Artwork copyright © 2008 by C&T Publishing, Inc.

Publisher: Amy Marson

Creative Director: Gailen Runge

Acquisitions Editor: Jan Grigsby

Editors: Kesel Wilson and Nichola Fortney

Technical Editors: Ellen Pahl and Robyn Gronning

Copyeditor/Proofreader: Wordfirm Inc.

Cover Designer: Kristen Yenche

Design Director: Kristy Zacharias

Book Designer: Kiera Lofgreen

Production Coordinator: Zinnia Heinzmann

Illustrator: Kirstie L. Pettersen

Photography by Luke Mulks and Diane Pedersen of C&T Publishing
unless otherwise noted

Published by C&T Publishing, Inc., P.O. Box 1456,
Lafayette, CA 94549

Attention Teachers: C&T Publishing, Inc., encourages you to use this book as a text for teaching. Contact us at 800-284-1114 or www.ctpub.com for more information about the C&T Teachers' Program.

We take great care to ensure that the information included in our products is accurate and presented in good faith, but no warranty is provided nor are results guaranteed. Having no control over the choices of materials or procedures used, neither the authors nor C&T Publishing, Inc., shall have any liability to any person or entity with respect to any loss or damage caused directly or indirectly by the information contained in this book. For your convenience, we post an up-to-date listing of corrections on our website (www.ctpub.com). If a correction is not already noted, please contact our customer service department at ctinfo@ctpub.com or at P.O. Box 1456, Lafayette, CA 94549.

Trademark (™) and registered trademark (®) names are used throughout this book. Rather than use the symbols with every occurrence of a trademark or registered trademark name, we are using the names only in the editorial fashion and to the benefit of the owner, with no intention of infringement.

Library of Congress Cataloging-in-Publication Data

Rosenthal, Maxine.

One-block wonders encore! : new shapes, multiple fabrics, out-of-this-world quilts / Maxine Rosenthal and Joy Pelzmann.

p. cm.

Summary: "A follow-up to One-Block Wonders, these quilts incorporate more fabrics. New content includes the much-anticipated instructions for making hollow cubes and instructions for letting the design elements fall into the border. Includes instructions for 6 projects."--Provided by publisher.

ISBN 978-1-57120-464-6 (paper trade : alk. paper)   39249684   12/08

1. Patchwork--Patterns. 2. Quilting. 3. Kaleidoscope quilts. I. Pelzmann, Joy. II. Title. III. Title: 1-block wonders encore!

TT835.R6738 2008

746.46'041--dc22

2007042376

Printed in China

10 9 8 7 6 5 4 3 2

Contents

Acknowledgments

At its very best, creativity is a collaborative process. We want to thank all our students for their perspective, their enthusiasm, and their ideas.

We also want to thank each other for the synergy of the shared process. Neither one of us alone could have created so much, so well, in so short a time. We challenged each other to move out of our comfort zone and to ask, "*What if*?"

Finally, we thank our families, who are always honest and always refreshing in response to our work.

Dedication
To Friendship

an introduction to hexagons

Starry Night, 55″ × 66″. Machine pieced by Joy Pelzmann. Quilted by Maxine Rosenthal.

Welcome to the next generation of *One-Block Wonders*. We have taken the basic hexagonal kaleidoscope and enhanced it with straightforward techniques that create powerful designs. These additional techniques produce design elements that amplify the impact of both the individual blocks and the overall quilt. You'll be surprised at how easy these techniques are and yet how complex they look to the observer. Once again, fabric is the key! Other new elements of this book include precise, complete directions for the creative process as well as project instructions for creating your own *One-Block Wonders*.

You will love this unusual method of designing and creating quilts. The primary fabric does the bulk of the work and defines your color palette. The hexagon blocks you create from this fabric ultimately form the foundation of your quilt, and, once all the blocks are created, you begin to design the final quilt on a design wall. After you are satisfied with your initial arrangement, you can choose from the techniques in this book to add to it. Because you haven't committed to a final design at this point, you can audition the elements found in the following chapters: will it be cubes, a banner border, an open slice, or a combination of elements? The possibilities are endless. Not only is designing with kaleidoscopes and cubes a forgiving process, but the elements covered in this book can also be used to address any design challenges you may encounter. We've taught our method to countless students, and we are confident that with this book, you will be able to create unique and original creations to be proud of.

It is hard to say exactly what size your quilt will be unless you follow the instructions for one of the projects at the ends of the chapters. The quilt size will depend on the design elements you add to the quilt; it may even become two quilts. It's your choice!

Supplies You Will Need

You probably already own all or most of the tools required to make the quilts in this book.

- Rotary cutting equipment: You will need a self-healing mat, long and short rulers, and a rotary cutter with a 45mm or 60mm blade. Inserting a new blade into the rotary cutter will ease the work of cutting six layers at once.

- A 60° ruler: This ruler is **mandatory** for creating cubes. We use the **Clearview Triangle** ruler (See *Resources*, page 79.) and the measurements for cubes are based on this ruler.

- Flower pins: These pins lie flat and do not shift when you are cutting.

- Sewing machine in good working order with a 1/4″ foot

- Thread

- Iron

- Design wall: This is **indispensable** for looking at your design from a distance. When you design on a floor, some elements are closer to your eye than others, whereas on a wall everything is equidistant. The ability to stand back and view your quilt makes it easier to see what is right and wrong with your design as you progress. A design wall is particularly helpful when you are selecting additional techniques to add elements to the quilt. You also get to see the quilt grow before your very eyes.

Choice of Fabrics

You can find tempting fabric while out shopping or while catalog shopping in your pajamas. Choosing your primary fabric is the first step. Choose fabric that features colors you love. If you like the colors of the fabric, you will enjoy making the quilt. Our favorite color is red. We rarely need to walk down the brown aisle in any fabric store.

Background

Select a fabric with a minimal amount of background. A fabric with too much background produces blocks with little design. A fabric with several small figures scattered on the background is not a good choice either.

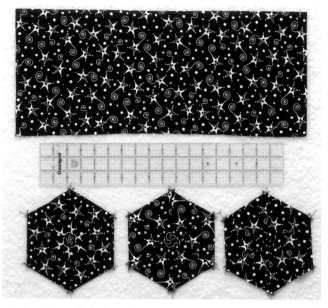

Fabric with small design elements makes less-interesting kaleidoscopic hexagons.

Sometimes background enhances the design. Movement, shading, or a secondary pattern can create more-interesting blocks. For example, fish in a raging sea will be better than flowers (or cowboys) on a black background.

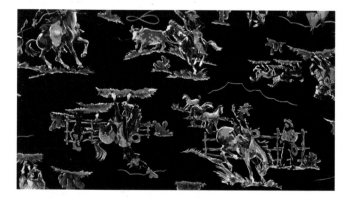

Background with movement versus plain background

Stripes versus Swirls

Stripes, especially stripes that run perpendicular or parallel to the selvage, require precise assembly techniques. Fabrics with stripes and straight lines also lack the movement and flow that make these quilts so effective. However, stripes can be used effectively in the border. We like the snap and power of these graphic elements as they play off the flowing nature of the kaleidoscopes, and putting them in the border of the quilt allows for that interplay.

Kaleidoscopes with straight lines are less interesting. Note that your eye is drawn to the imperfection of the assembly of the block above.

Swirled designs work well in kaleidoscopes because the swirls will never be expected to meet at the seam.

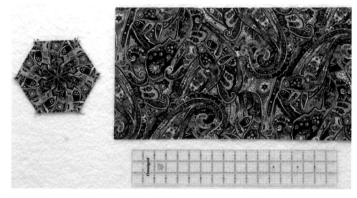

Kaleidoscopes from swirled designs are more exciting.

When sewn into kaleidoscope blocks, fabrics with curving elements create the illusion of movement, producing blocks with drama and motion. For example, leaves with scalloped edges and curling tips have this movement. Although any leaf can be beautiful in kaleidoscope blocks, one that is larger and has more curls is more visually interesting.

Straight-sided leaf versus leaf with movement

Large-scale print and the kaleidoscopes it produces

Large Is Good

The larger the print, the less the finished blocks will look like the original fabric. This is the result you want! It's fun to have people say, "I can't believe this fabric produced this quilt. No way!"

Notice that the designs in the fabric below repeat both horizontally and vertically. As long as the design repeat isn't too short or too frequent, the resulting kaleidoscopes can be very interesting.

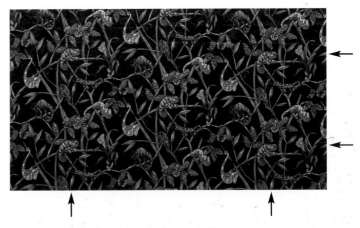

Designs repeating horizontally and vertically

A short design repeat is good for a small project, such as a baby quilt. For example, a 12″ repeat means that you are buying at least 2 yards of fabric (12″ × 6 repeats = 72″). This yardage would not be enough for a bed-size quilt. For a bed-size quilt, look for a larger print, one with a 24″ repeat. We tend to prefer large, dramatic prints, but that is a taste consideration, not an absolute requirement.

Fabrics with large animals or flowers, or even people, make interesting kaleidoscopes because they contain recognizable elements, such as fish tails, lions' noses, car tires, or the hand of a cowboy waving as he rides a bucking bronco. Have fun and experiment!

Fabric with too many colors

Tip *When shopping for fabric, bring two mirrors. Arrange the mirrors in a V shape and move them around the fabric to get an idea of the kaleidoscopes it will form.*

Mirrors on fabric

Colors

Limit the number of colors in the fabric. Designing with two or three colors is much easier than designing with eight or nine. The *Starry Night* quilt, page 4, includes variations of one color in the background and limits the remaining contrasting colors to yellow and orange. Even though there is a lot of blue background, the wave pattern creates subtly varied kaleidoscopes.

Sometimes you'll find a fabric that is so gorgeous you can't pass it up. Just keep in mind that breaking the color rule will create design challenges later in the process.

Yardage Amounts

How much fabric should you buy? *The only rule is that you need six repeats of your fabric to make a hexagon.* The size of the quilt depends not only on how much fabric you buy but also on how many hexagon blocks you eventually use in the quilt. The good news is that you don't have to worry about leftover fabric. Use it on the back of your quilt or add it to your stash.

Measure the Length of the Repeat

Measure along the selvage from the start of a design element to the point where the element appears again. This is the length of the repeat. Most fabric is printed with some multiple of 4″ as the length of the repeat. Your repeat must be at least 8″ to give enough variety to the kaleidoscopes. If you choose an 8″ repeat, you will need 6 repeats; 6 × 8″ = 48″ or 1$\frac{1}{3}$ yards. See the table on the next page for yardages needed for various repeats.

Try including some of your chosen fabric "whole" in the quilt, even if it's only on the back. Turning the quilt over and showing people the fabric that the quilt came from is so much fun. Including $\frac{1}{2}$ yard of the original fabric uncut brings you up to 1$\frac{7}{8}$ yards for a fabric with an 8″ repeat, which still will make only a small project. If the repeat is short, you can opt to buy twelve repeats instead of six. *Larger prints usually have a 24″ repeat—this is the type of fabric we typically choose.* Five yards of fabric makes a comfortable lap quilt, and, depending on the borders used, the quilt can grow to any size.

Other Guidelines for Fabric

The wonderful thing about making these quilts is that no fabric preparation is required. *Do not prewash the fabric.* Prewashing removes the sizing and can distort the fabric. You can begin cutting into your fabric as soon as you get it home.

Do not buy fabric from more than one bolt. Sometimes you find the perfect fabric, but there is only a yard or two on the bolt. Don't be tempted to search the Internet or buy some of the fabric at another store. There is no guarantee that the colors or print of the pattern will be exactly the same from bolt to bolt.

YARDAGE REQUIREMENTS AND HEXAGON YIELDS

LENGTH OF REPEAT	LENGTH OF 6 REPEATS	YARDAGE NEEDED	YARDAGE + 1/2 YARD FOR QUILT BACK	YIELD OF 6" HEXAGON BLOCKS
8″	48″	$1\frac{1}{3}$ yards	$1\frac{7}{8}$ yards	36–38
12″	72″	2 yards	$2\frac{1}{2}$ yards	54–57
16″	96″	$2\frac{2}{3}$ yards	$3\frac{1}{4}$ yards	72–76
24″	144″	4 yards	$4\frac{1}{2}$ yards	108–114

Chapter 2
creating hexagons

Wisterious, 71½" × 54". Machine pieced by Elizabeth Vikla of Blue Bamboo. Quilted by Theresa Francisco.

Finding and Cutting Repeats

Fabric, selvage to selvage, is about 42˝ wide and we will refer to that as the width. The length of the pattern repeat determines the lengths of the cuts you make; you need to cut six of these lengths from your fabric to make the hexagons. A 24˝ repeat means that you will make a cut every 24˝. An 8˝ repeat means that you will make a cut every 8˝. However, if you buy twelve repeats of an 8˝ repeat in order to make more blocks for a larger quilt, make each cut 16˝ long.

Leave the fabric folded as it came off the bolt (selvage to selvage). Lay out your fabric and look along the cut edge to identify a design element that will be easy to recognize when it next appears. Move along either the fold or the selvages and look for that design element again. If the length of the repeat is short and you have purchased twelve, rather than six repeats, move along to the *second* repeat of this design element.

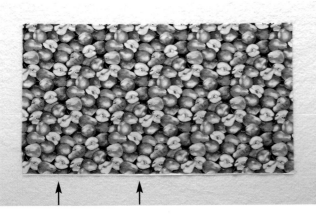

Single repeat

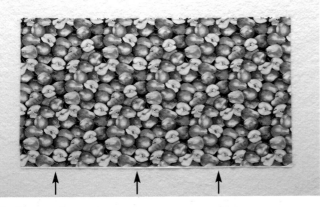

Double repeat

Cutting Repeats

1. After you've identified a design element close to the cut edge of the fabric, use a rotary cutter and ruler to cut through the *folded* fabric at the place where this design element appears again. Put this piece aside. *NOTE:* This is a rough initial cut. You are not trying for perfection yet.

2. Cut the next repeat the same way, so that the second cut ends at the same place in the design as the first cut. Stack this second cut on the first cut. Continue until you have six repeats cut.

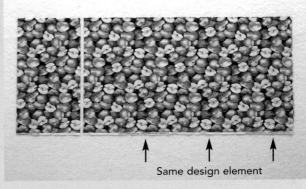

Same design element

Cut the next repeats.

3. You now have six cuts of fabric that are about the same. Unfold each cut and iron it to remove the crease from the center fold. Stack all the fabric pieces, without folding, making sure the design elements are facing in the same direction. Do not worry if the pieces are not exactly the same or if one is a little longer than the others.

Aligning the Fabric

You will insert six flower pins into the fabric pieces, as described in the following steps.

- 2 along one selvage
- 1 on each cut edge, approximately at the center fold
- 2 along the other selvage

1. Starting at a selvage corner, find a point where 2 design elements intersect. This point should be about 1″ from the cut edge of the fabric and about 1″ from the selvage. Do not use the *end* of a design element as your point. The end of an element may not always be printed on the fabric, but where design elements cross, they will always cross. Put a flower pin straight into the intersection point.

Intersection of design elements

2. Lift the top piece of fabric with the pin sticking into it to reveal the next layer of fabric. Push the pin into the spot on the next piece of fabric where *the same 2 design elements intersect*. Repeat for the remaining layers. Count the layers as you go. It is easy to miss a layer because it was folded in or did not reach the edge.

3. Leave the pin sticking straight up in the fabric layers. Repeat Steps 1 and 2 on the other cut edge along the same selvage.

Insert two pins along selvage.

4. There are now 2 pins sticking straight into the fabric pieces, one at either edge of one selvage. Hold the shaft of each pin between the index and middle fingers of each hand and press the top edge of each flower pin with your thumb. It looks awkward. It is awkward. But you really have a grip on the pins.

How to hold a pin

Holding two pins

5. Being sure to hold the pins, let the fabric hang loose and give the layers a little shake with your hands to straighten them. *NOTE:* If you prewashed the fabric, the layers will stick together and not shake out as freely. While holding the pins, give the fabric layers a gentle tug away from the center. Aligning the fabric is the hardest task.

6. Lay the fabric stack down. Check along the selvage edges and the cut edges to ensure that the design elements in the layers are aligned. Spread apart the layers of fabric to see whether the design elements match.

Fabric aligned

10. Move along the fabric to where the fold line was. Put a flower pin in straight along each cut edge as described in Steps 1 and 2. Again, find an easily recognizable place where two design elements of a pattern intersect. These 2 pins will stick straight up. Hold on to them as described in Step 4 and give the fabric a little shake, tugging outward to align all the layers.

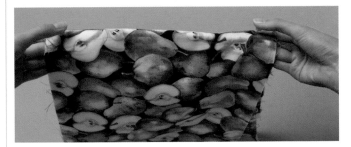

Hold two pins at center along fold line.

7. With the fabric stack resting on the table, hold the shaft of one of the pins so the index and middle fingers of one hand are behind the fabric and your thumb is resting on the front of the fabric. *Do not turn this pin to secure the fabric.* Turning the pin would ruin the alignment you have just worked so hard to perfect. With your other hand, insert another flower pin into the fabric layers so that it slides in almost parallel to the fabric. When inserting this pin, make sure it is at such a slanted angle that the design elements remain aligned. *If you let go of the original pin, it should still stand straight.* If the first pin does not stand straight, pull out the second flower pin and reinsert it, trying not to shift any of the layers as you do so. On the front side of the fabric, there should be a long space of fabric between the points where the pin entered and exited; on the back side, there should be very little pin showing. This indicates that the pin is slanted enough so as not to alter the alignment of the fabric layers.

11. Replace each pin with a flower pin, as described in Steps 7 and 8.

12. Repeat Steps 1–9 along the other selvage. For this step it is easiest to turn the fabric around so the bottom selvage is at the top. The fabric is now perfectly aligned and you have 6 pins holding the layers in place. You can confirm this by looking at the print of the fabric along the cut edges to see that the design elements line up.

13. Use a rotary cutter and ruler to cut a straight edge along one side of the fabric stack from selvage to selvage. Only one edge needs to be cut straight. If the edge is not perfectly straight, that's OK. You will be cutting small triangles, so you don't need the edge to be exactly perpendicular to the selvage. Once you have aligned the fabric layers and cut the straight edge, you can relax and enjoy the rest of the process.

First pin standing straight

8. Remove the pin that is sticking straight up beside the new pin.

9. Repeat Steps 7 and 8 at the other side of the selvage. You now have 2 pins securing the fabric.

Cut a straight edge.

Cutting Triangles for Hexagons

Generally, the length of the six repeats that you cut will be a multiple of 4″. We are not perfect, and don't even want to try to be, so we cut our strips for hexagons at 3¾″, rather than 4″. This gives us a little breathing room when cutting, and it reduces the possibility of cutting identical strips.

1. Beginning at the trimmed edge of the stacked and pinned fabric, cut strips 3¾″ wide. As you pass a pin, put another one into the remaining chunk of fabric.

Tip

As you cut a strip with a pin in it, remember to add a pin to the remaining chunk of the fabric to maintain the alignment. Pinning this way will hold the uncut pieces in place.

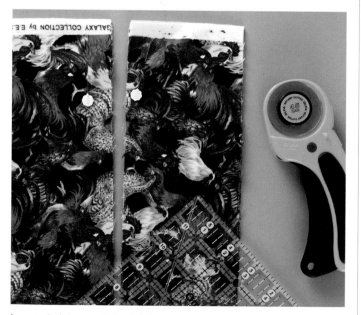

Insert pin into remaining fabric.

2. Lay out the 3¾″ strips horizontally, keeping the 6 layers neatly aligned.

3. Place the 60° Clearview Triangle ruler close to the selvage, with the ruler's 3¾″ line at one cut edge and the point of the triangle at the other cut edge.

3¾″ line

Align 60° triangle ruler on fabric.

4. Cut along the right side of the triangle ruler and then gently position a smaller rectangular ruler against the left edge of the triangle ruler. Remove the triangle ruler and make a right-handed cut. We know that some people can cut at awkward angles or use their non-dominant hand, but we can't so we need a way to keep our cuts right-handed.

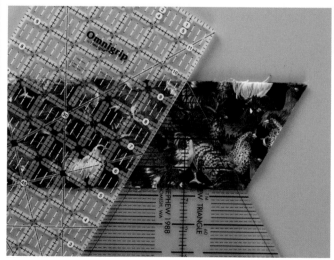

Line up small ruler.

5. For the next cut, place the 60° ruler on the strip as before, skipping the upside-down triangle. Be sure that the 3¾″ line at the right edge of the ruler is against the right edge of the fabric, that the point of the ruler is on the top edge of the fabric, and that the lower edge of the fabric is along the

3¾″ line on the ruler. Make a right-handed cut along the triangle ruler. Again, place a smaller rectangular ruler along the left edge of the triangle ruler, remove the triangle ruler, and cut again. You just cut 2 sets of triangles with one placement—2 for the price of 1. Keep each stack of triangles together. Each stack of 6 will make 1 hexagon block.

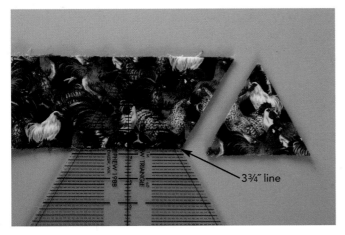

Cut next triangles.

Each 42″ strip of fabric will yield 18 or 19 triangles, and each stack of triangles will make 1 hexagon block. Because you are cutting 6 layers at once, you'll have plenty of kaleidoscopic hexagon blocks to play with. Each strip will produce a different array of triangles, possibly even different colors, depending on your fabric. Handle the triangles carefully to avoid stretching the bias edges.

Sewing Half Hexagons

1. Keep the straight of grain to the outside edge of the hexagon. The straight of grain can be most easily seen on the wrong side of the fabric, where you can see the threads that did not get any dye.

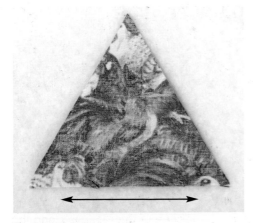

Straight of grain

2. Sew sets of 3 triangles together to create *half hexagons*. Press the seams open—**always**. Some people are concerned about working with bias edges. We are not; the extra bit of stretch helps us to make corners line up with one another.

3. *Pin the half hexagons together, but do not sew them into hexagons.* This will enable you to sew the quilt together in rows without having to sew set-in seams. Instead of pinning as the seam would be sewn, with right sides together, pin the halves together with the edge of one overlapping the edge of its mate. This way, the hexagons lie flat when put on the design wall and the 2 halves stay together. You don't want to mix up hexagons.

Pin half hexagons together.

4. Put your pinned hexagons on your design wall and get ready to play!

Chapter 3
cubes

Wild Mustangs, 76" × 62". Machine pieced and quilted by Joy Pelzmann.

Cubes can be made from hexagons by creating the illusion of dimension. This illusion is achieved by making the eye believe there is a light source. This light source must be consistent throughout the quilt to be believable, so the shading must be the same for each cube.

For this technique you need light, intermediate, and dark value fabrics. We will use the word *intermediate* to denote value and the word *medium* to define size.

 **Tip** An intermediate fabric in one cube may be the dark fabric in another. Do not place these cubes next to each other in the quilt, as this would destroy the illusion of a light source.

For the cubes, choose fabrics that will work well when placed in the same quilt with your kaleidoscope hexagons. *The cube fabrics need to read as solids.* You may also want to use some of the original kaleidoscope fabric. Because your kaleidoscope fabric does not read as a solid, take care in selecting its location in the quilt, as well as what parts of the fabric you cut.

Strip with light and dark areas

The first question you need to ask yourself is whether you want these cubes to blend into your quilt and be hidden or if you want them to stand out in relief. Your choice will depend in part on your kaleidoscopic fabric and your personal taste. Here is your chance to try out some of those luscious batiks you've been drooling over but couldn't quite place in any other quilt. Remember that gradation of hand dyes you just couldn't resist at the quilt show? This is the perfect place for them. Many shades of the same color add interest to the quilt, and it is not unusual for us to use fifteen or twenty fabrics in our cubes. Fat quarters are perfect for this purpose.

THE FOLLOWING DIRECTIONS ARE LIKE A RECIPE.

Read through them, collect your ingredients, and then begin mixing. The measurements given will produce 6″-finished hexagons, the same size as your kaleidoscope hexagons. All seams are $1/4$″. Press all the seams open and do not trim off points. Remember, you are making half hexagons. Do not sew the half hexagons together—simply pin them together for easy assembly of the quilt later on.

Solid Cubes

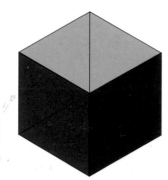

This cube is one you may have made before. We've included it here to establish shading and to show how the block goes together to make a basic cube. Each side of this cube appears as a solid surface, and it is made of six unpieced triangles.

1. Cut 3³⁄₄″-wide strips of light, intermediate, and dark value fabrics. Note: These need not be of the same color.

2. Cut two 3³⁄₄″ triangles of each fabric (see *Cutting Triangles for Hexagons*, page 14).

3. Sew 2 dark triangles together and 2 intermediate triangles together to create 2 diamond units.

4. Place a light triangle at the top of each diamond made in Step 3, as shown.

Placement of light fabric triangles

5. Pin the light triangles to the diamonds, aligning the raw edges. Take care to sew along the correct seam; it's easy to sew the wrong side of the triangle if you haven't pinned it first.

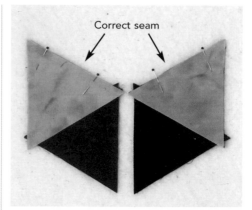

Sew correct side of light triangle.

6. Sew the seams and press them open. *Do not sew these half hexagons together*. Trust us—this makes it easier to complete the quilt later. Put this cube on the design wall. It will be your reference for those that follow.

> **Tip**
>
> *Remember that the light fabric is on the top, the dark on the right, and the intermediate on the left. This placement reflects the location of the light source, and consistency is important: the imagined light source is always in the upper left of the quilt in these directions.*

Trapezoids as Building Blocks

A regular trapezoid looks like the base of an equilateral triangle with the pointed top removed. Cutting trapezoid pieces using the Clearview Triangle ruler is easy. The cutting sizes in all the following directions correspond to the numbering system running down the center of the Clearview Triangle ruler. *Throughout the book, all trapezoids are cut from 1¹⁄₂″ strips of fabric.* When sewn together, the small, medium, and large trapezoids create one equilateral triangle.

● The **small** trapezoid is cut by aligning the lower edge of the strip of fabric with the 1³⁄₄″ line of the ruler. On the small trapezoid, the point of the Clearview Triangle ruler sticks out just beyond the edge of the strip. This is correct. When the block is finished and all seams are sewn, this piece will be a triangle.

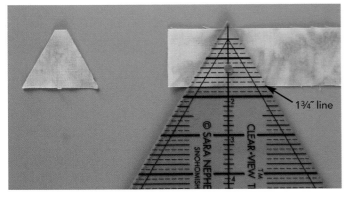
Small trapezoid

● The **medium** trapezoid is cut by aligning the lower edge of the strip of fabric with the $2^{3}/4''$ line of the ruler.

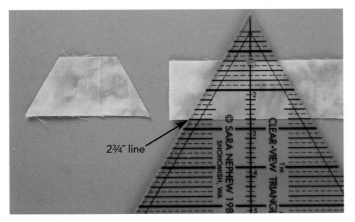
Medium trapezoid

● The **large** trapezoid is cut by aligning the lower edge of the strip of fabric with the $3^{3}/4''$ line of the ruler.

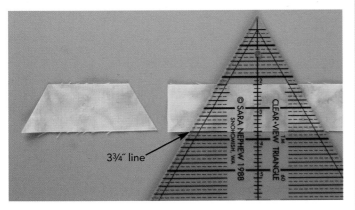
Large trapezoid

When sewing the trapezoids together, you may think they cannot possibly fit. However, when they are placed in position with right sides together, the $^{1}/4''$ seam will be perfectly aligned in the notch.

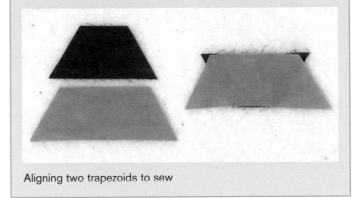
Aligning two trapezoids to sew

Cube in a Corner

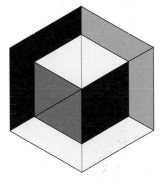

In our classes, we have referred to this as a *hollowed-out cube*. However, to better distinguish it from hollow cubes (beginning on page 22), we are calling it *cube in a corner*.

1. Cut a $1^{1}/2''$ strip and a $2^{3}/4''$ strip from each of 3 fabrics: a light, an intermediate, and a dark.

2. From the $2^{3}/4''$ strips, cut 2 triangles each of the light, intermediate, and dark fabrics (see *Cutting Triangles for Hexagons*, page 14).

3. From the 1½˝ strips, cut 3¾˝ (large) trapezoids: 2 each of the light, intermediate, and dark fabrics. Arrange the fabric pieces as shown. Sew the trapezoids to the triangles (see *Trapezoids as Building Blocks*, page 18). Press the seams open.

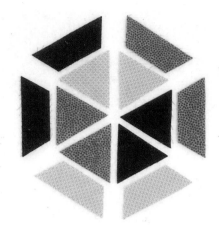

Exploded cube in a corner

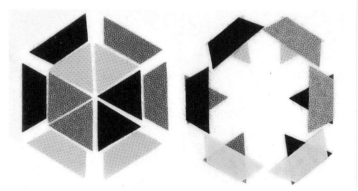

Sew trapezoids to triangles.

4. Sew the triangles together to create the half hexagons (see *Sewing Half Hexagons*, page 15). Press the seams open.

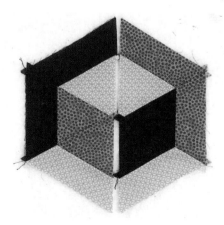

Completed half hexagons

5. Pin the half hexagons together. Place them on the design wall and step away. You now have a cube in a corner.

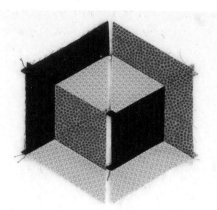

Cube in a corner (also known as hollowed-out cube)

6. Turn this block upside down and step away again. Notice how the look of the block changes entirely? You can easily use this difference to add visual interest to your quilt.

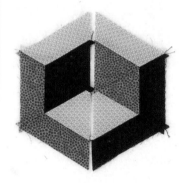
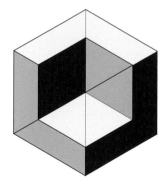

Upside down cube in a corner

Solid Cube Open at One Side

What do you see when you look into a box? If you look into the open dark side, the darkest part of the opening is toward the center on the inside. We can re-create this shading by using three different dark colors.

The lightest dark fabric must be darker than the intermediate fabric.

Up until now we have been using triangles made of one or two fabrics, but now we will create shaded triangles pieced from three trapezoids.

We are only including directions for a cube open on the dark side. To open the cube on the light side (top), replace the light triangles with two shaded triangles pieced from three lights (the darkest light should be lighter than the intermediate). To open the cube on the intermediate side, replace the intermediate triangles with two shaded triangles pieced from three intermediates (the lightest intermediate should be darker than the light, and the darkest intermediate should be lighter than the dark).

Cube Open on the Dark Side

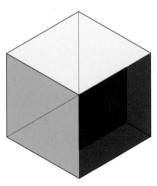

1. To create 2 shaded triangles use 3 shades of dark fabric; cut a $1\frac{1}{2}$″ strip from each fabric.

2. Cut 2 small ($1\frac{3}{4}$″) trapezoids from the darkest dark fabric (see *Trapezoids as Building Blocks*, page 18).

3. Cut 2 medium ($2\frac{3}{4}$″) trapezoids from the intermediate dark fabric.

4. Cut 2 large ($3\frac{3}{4}$″) trapezoids from the lightest of the dark fabrics.

5. Cut two $3\frac{3}{4}$″ triangles each of the light and intermediate fabrics (see *Cutting Triangles for Hexagons*, page 14).

6. Arrange the fabric pieces as shown. Sew the trapezoids together to form triangles. Sew the triangles together. Be sure to match the seams exactly; the points must line up, so take your time. Accuracy promotes the illusion.

Exploded cube open on dark side

7. Sew the half hexagons together (see *Sewing Half Hexagons*, page 15). Pin the halves together, place them on the design wall, and admire.

Completed cube open on dark side

Hollow Cubes

This block design was developed by Sara Nephew. We use these hollow cube blocks to add interest to the quilt.

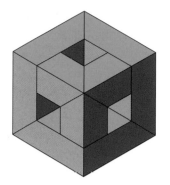

What would you see if there were a window in each wall of a cube? As we look at the cube from the front, the top window exposes a glimpse of both side walls. Through the windows on the sides, you see the other side and the floor of the cube. A light, an intermediate, and a dark fabric are all you need for this amazing illusion.

As you cut your pieces, lay them out carefully following the block photograph given with the instructions. Being systematic reduces confusion and error. As you get more comfortable making these cubes, you will find a system that works for you.

Our system is analogous to the face of a clock. We begin at twelve o'clock and move in a clockwise direction.

- Place the smallest trapezoid on the medium trapezoid and sew the two together.

- Continue around the cube, sewing each small trapezoid to a medium trapezoid. Press the seams open.

- Place these units back in their correct position and sew a large trapezoid to each of the triangles you just completed. Press the seams open and position the units as before.

- You are now ready to complete the half hollow cubes.

The Three Rules of Hollow Cubes

1. Each cube is *always* composed of light, intermediate, and dark fabrics. It is this shading that defines a cube.

2. Each cube is made of 6 triangles.

3. Each triangle of the cube is *always* pieced with a $1^{3/4}''$ trapezoid (a triangle when finished), a $2^{3/4}''$ trapezoid, and a $3^{3/4}''$ trapezoid, which are labeled as small, medium, and large, respectively.

The Triangles of Hollow Cubes

There are two basic methods for piecing triangles that are not made of a solid piece of fabric: the "V-shape method" and the "stripe method." Each method also has a corresponding rule.

- **V-shape rule:** In the V-shape method, the medium and large trapezoids are always the same color, and the smallest trapezoid is always a different color.

- **Stripe rule:** In the stripe method, the smallest trapezoid is always the same color as the largest trapezoid, and the center trapezoid is always a different color.

V-shape triangle and stripe triangle

How you place the $1^{3/4}''$ trapezoid does not matter. The cut off-point will fall into a seam. In the finished piece it will appear as a triangle.

It is the use of light, intermediate, and dark fabrics combined with the two basic triangle shapes that makes hollow cubes look hollow. These basic shapes can be arranged in several different ways to produce completely unique-looking hollow cubes. Learning the secrets of the hollow cube adds an amazing array of design elements to your toolbox.

Basic Hollow Cubes

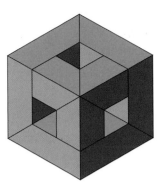

The basic hollow cube is made of six V triangles. Two V triangles with outside "arms" (medium and large trapezoids) of the same color are placed together to form a diamond. When the block is completed, each diamond becomes a side of the cube with a square "hole" in it.

1. Cut 1½˝ strips of light, intermediate, and dark fabrics.

2. Cut 6 small (1¾˝) trapezoids: 2 light, 2 intermediate, and 2 dark (see *Trapezoids as Building Blocks*, page 18).

3. Cut 6 medium (2¾˝) trapezoids: 2 light, 2 intermediate, and 2 dark.

4. Cut 6 large (3¾˝) trapezoids: 2 light, 2 intermediate, and 2 dark.

5. Arrange the fabric pieces as shown.

Exploded hollow cube

6. Study the exploded block in the photograph above to make sure you place all the trapezoids correctly.

7. Sew each small trapezoid to a medium trapezoid to form a triangle. Press the seams open.

8. Sew the large trapezoid to either side of the newly formed triangle. Remember that you want to create the V-shape.

9. Sew the two V triangles with the intermediate-value sides together, forming a diamond with the small triangles touching. Match the seam intersections of the inside triangles carefully because an inaccurate match will be visually noticeable. This is the place for accuracy. We insert a pin vertically at the point where the seams will intersect; once we have a perfect match, we insert a pin horizontally on either side of the vertical pin. Sew the 2 V triangles with the dark-value sides together the same way. Press the seams open.

10. Add the V-shape with light-value sides and the intermediate center to the dark-edged diamond along the side with the intermediate inner triangle. Add the V-shape with light-value edges and the dark center to the intermediate-edged diamond along the side with the dark inner triangle.

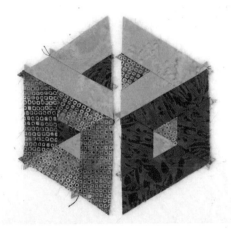

Add light V-shapes.

11. Pin the 2 halves together, put the unit on the design wall, and admire.

Completed hollow cube

Hollow Cubes Sliced Open

These cubes all have two stripe triangles and four V triangles. The stripe triangles create the slice and the V's create the hollow. Remember to press the seams open.

Hollow Cube with Slice on Left

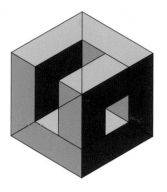

What do you see if there is a window in the right wall of the cube and the left side has an open slice? As you look at the cube from the top, you see an open slice on the left. You see into the cube through the slice as well as through the window on the right. Once again, this illusion is accomplished with a light, an intermediate, and a dark fabric. The light fabric is the mottled batik, and the medium fabric is the dotted batik. The value contrast is subtle, but adequate.

1. Cut $1^1/2^″$ strips of light, intermediate, and dark fabrics.

2. Cut 6 small ($1^3/4^″$) trapezoids: 3 light and 3 intermediate (see *Trapezoids as Building Blocks*, page 18).

3. Cut 6 medium ($2^3/4^″$) trapezoids: 1 light, 1 intermediate, and 4 dark.

4. Cut 6 large ($3^3/4^″$) trapezoids: 2 light, 2 intermediate, and 2 dark.

5. Arrange the fabric pieces as shown below.

Exploded cube with slice on left

6. Study the exploded block in the photograph following Step 5 to make sure you place the trapezoids correctly.

7. Sew each small trapezoid to a medium trapezoid to form triangles.

8. Referring to the exploded block photograph, add the larger trapezoids to form 4 V triangles and 2 stripe triangles. Remember the V-shape rule—the medium and large trapezoids should be the same color. Follow the stripe rule for the others—the larger trapezoid will be the same color as the small triangle.

9. Arrange the triangles following the exploded block photograph. Sew 3 of the triangles together to create a half hexagon; sew the remaining 3 triangles together to create the other half hexagon. Pin the halves together, put the hexagon on the design wall, and admire.

Completed half hexagons

Completed hollow cube with slice on left

Hollow Cube with Slice on Right

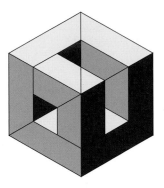

What do you see if there is a window in the left wall of the cube and the right side has an open slice? As you look at the cube from the top, you see an open slice on the right. You see into the cube through the slice as well as through the window on the left. Once again, this illusion is accomplished with a light, an intermediate, and a dark fabric.

1. Cut one 1½˝ strip each of light, intermediate, and dark fabrics.

2. Cut 6 small (1¾˝) trapezoids: 3 light and 3 dark (see *Trapezoids as Building Blocks*, page 18).

3. Cut 6 medium (2¾˝) trapezoids: 1 light, 4 intermediate, and 1 dark.

4. Cut 6 large (3¾˝) trapezoids: 2 light, 2 intermediate, and 2 dark.

5. Arrange the fabric pieces as shown below.

Exploded hollow cube with slice on right

6. Study the exploded block in the photograph above to make sure you place the trapezoids correctly.

7. Sew each small trapezoid to a medium trapezoid to form triangles.

8. Referring to the exploded block photograph, add the larger trapezoids to form 4 V triangles and 2 stripe triangles. Remember the V-shape rule—the medium and large trapezoids should be the same color. Follow the stripe rule for the others—the larger trapezoid will be the same color as the small triangle.

9. Arrange the triangles following the exploded block photograph. Sew 3 of the triangles together to create a half hexagon; sew the remaining 3 triangles together to create the other half hexagon. Pin the halves together, put the hexagon on the design wall, and admire.

Completed half hexagons

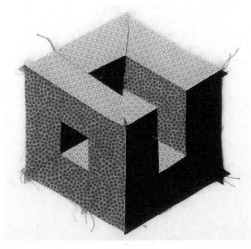

Completed hollow cube with slice on right

Hollow Cube with Slice on Front

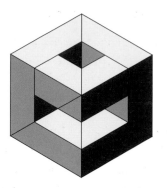

What do you see if there is a window in the top of the cube and an open slice in the front? As you look at the cube from the top, you see into the cube through the window. You can also see the floor of the cube through the open slice. Once again, this illusion is accomplished with a light, an intermediate, and a dark fabric.

1. Cut one $1\frac{1}{2}$″ strip each of light, intermediate, and dark fabrics.

2. Cut six small ($1\frac{3}{4}$″) trapezoids: 3 intermediate and 3 dark (see *Trapezoids as Building Blocks*, page 18).

3. Cut six medium ($2\frac{3}{4}$″) trapezoids: 4 light, 1 intermediate, and 1 dark

4. Cut six large ($3\frac{3}{4}$″) trapezoids: 2 light, 2 intermediate, and 2 dark

5. Arrange the fabric pieces as shown below.

6. Study the exploded block in the photograph following Step 5 to make sure you place the trapezoids correctly.

7. Sew each small trapezoid to a medium trapezoid to form triangles.

8. Referring to the exploded block photograph, add the larger trapezoids to form 4 V triangles and 2 stripe triangles. Remember the V-shape rule—the medium and large trapezoids should be the same color. Follow the stripe rule for the others—the larger trapezoid will be the same color as the small triangle.

9. Arrange the triangles following the exploded block photograph. Sew 3 of the triangles together to create a half hexagon; sew the remaining 3 triangles together to create the other half hexagon. Pin the halves together, put the hexagon on the design wall, and admire.

Completed half hexagons

Exploded hollow cube with slice on front

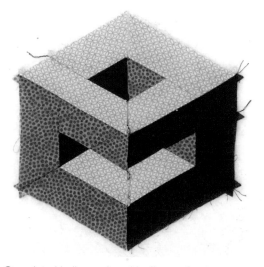

Completed hollow cube with slice on front

Cube within a Cube

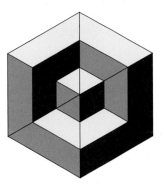

What do you see if there is a cube sitting in the corner of a larger cube? You see the back walls and the floor of the larger cube and a small cube resting in the back corner. Once again, this illusion is accomplished with a light, an intermediate, and a dark fabric. The cube within a cube is made from six stripe triangles.

1. Cut one $1\frac{1}{2}$˝ strip each of light, intermediate, and dark fabrics.

2. Cut 6 small ($1\frac{3}{4}$˝) trapezoids: 2 light, 2 intermediate, and 2 dark (see *Trapezoids as Building Blocks*, page 18).

3. Cut 6 medium ($2\frac{3}{4}$˝) trapezoids: 2 light, 2 intermediate, and 2 dark.

4. Cut 6 large ($3\frac{3}{4}$˝) trapezoids: 2 light, 2 intermediate, and 2 dark.

5. Arrange the fabric pieces as shown below.

Exploded cube within a cube

6. Study the exploded block in the photograph following Step 5 to make sure you place the trapezoids correctly.

7. Sew each small trapezoid to a medium trapezoid to form triangles. Add the larger trapezoids to form 6 stripe triangles. Remember the stripe rule—the larger trapezoid will be the same color as the small triangle.

8. Arrange the triangles following the exploded block photograph. Sew 3 of the triangles together to create a half hexagon; sew the remaining 3 triangles together to create the other half hexagon. Pin the halves together, put the hexagon on the design wall, and admire.

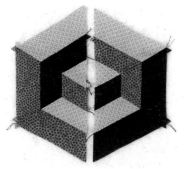
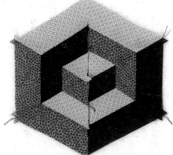

Completed half hexagons   Completed cube within a cube

You can turn this cube upside down to create a completely different illusion.

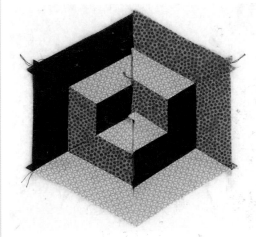

Upside down cube within a cube

Designing with Cubes and Hexagons

As you audition your quilt on the wall, some areas will work better for you than others. Cubes to the rescue! They can solve awkward transition problems and bring interest and movement to the quilt.

Because there are two authors of this book, there are two approaches to design. Maxine makes cubes as she sees the need for them. In contrast, Joy makes many cubes and then uses the ones that suit her project best.

Our experience has taught us that a cluster of cubes creates a stronger illusion than just one poor lonely cube. Joy sees water flowing through the cubes and places her cubes to enhance this movement. Even though these designs are abstract, each one tells a story.

The photo below is an example of a beginning point. On the design wall, we've arranged and are auditioning an array of kaleidoscopes we find pleasing.

We found several places where the transition was not as smooth as it could be. We covered those places with cubes, hollow and otherwise, and then added a few more for interest. This organic process always creates wonderful and stunning results.

Completed design including cubes, hollow and otherwise

Initial quilt design

One-of-a-Kind Quilt with Cubes

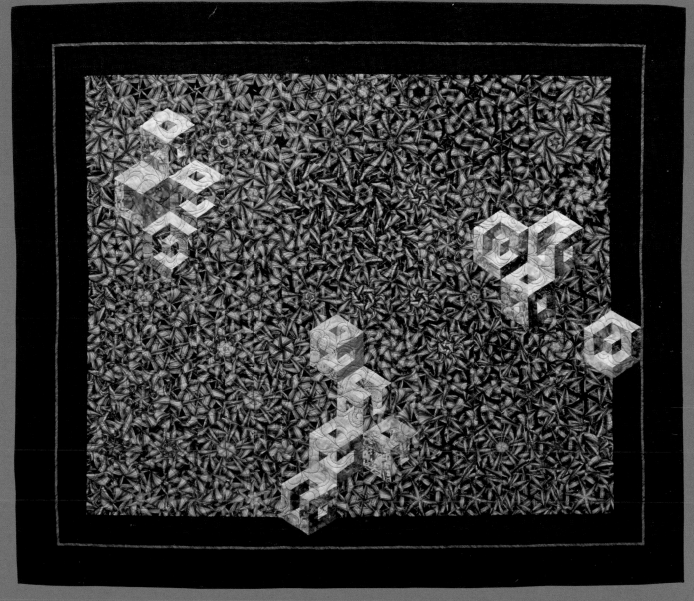

Sky's the Limit, 72″ × 60½″. Machine pieced and quilted by Joy Pelzmann.

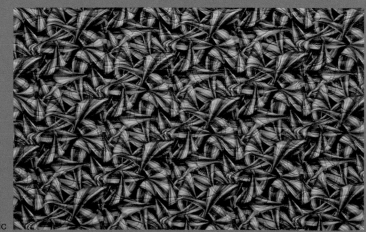

Original fabric

Materials

$4^{1}/_2$ yards of fabric for hexagon blocks (6 repeats plus $^{1}/_2$ yard to include in the backing)

A variety of coordinating fabrics in light, intermediate, and dark values for cubes

Borders and binding fabrics: $2^{1}/_2$ yards

Accent-border fabric: $^{1}/_4$ yard

Backing: $3^{3}/_4$ yards*

Batting: 76˝ × 65˝

*This quantity assumes you will include $^{1}/_2$ yard of the original fabric in the backing.

● ● ●

BEFORE YOU BEGIN: Refer to *Creating Hexagons*, page 10, for details on cutting repeats, aligning fabrics, cutting triangles, and sewing half hexagons.

Cutting

Block Fabric

1. Divide the fabric into 6 identical repeats.

2. Align all 6 layers exactly.

3. Trim one edge of the 6 layers and cut 6 strips $3^{3}/_4$˝ × the width of the fabric.

4. Using the Clearview Triangle ruler, cut $3^{3}/_4$˝ triangles through all 6 layers. Keep the triangles stacked together.

Border and Binding Fabrics

1. For the inner border, cut 7 strips $3^{1}/_2$˝ × the width of the fabric.

2. For the accent border, cut 7 strips $^{3}/_4$˝ × the width of the fabric.

3. For the outer border, cut 7 strips $4^{1}/_2$˝ × the width of the fabric.

4. For the binding, cut 7 strips $2^{1}/_2$˝ × the width of the fabric.

Sewing and Design

1. Sew the triangles into half hexagons, pressing the seams open. Pin the halves together. You will have anywhere from 108–114 blocks. You will need approximately 80–90 blocks to make the quilt as shown.

2. Arrange the blocks on a design wall in 9 rows of 9 blocks each. Add half blocks to the sides to fill in.

3. Play with the design and decide what types of cubes you want to incorporate into your quilt. Refer to *Cubes*, page 16, for specific cutting and sewing instructions for each type. Add cubes wherever they seem appropriate to you.

4. Assemble the quilt top by sewing the half hexagons together in vertical rows. Refer to *Hexagons or Cubes Falling Out of the Quilt*, page 68, for instructions on completing the inner border where cubes extend outside the quilt center.

5. Trim the top edge of the quilt.

Finishing

1. Measure your quilt vertically through the center. Use this measurement to cut 1 strip of the inner-border fabric, piecing as needed. Sew the strip to the left side of the quilt.

2. Measure your quilt horizontally through the center, including the borders. Piece and cut strips of inner-border fabric to the measured length; attach the inner border to the top of the quilt.

3. Repeat the measuring process to add the accent border and outer border to the quilt.

4. Make a backing. Quilt and bind.

Red Toile, 65″ × 73¹/₂″. Machine pieced and quilted by Maxine Rosenthal.

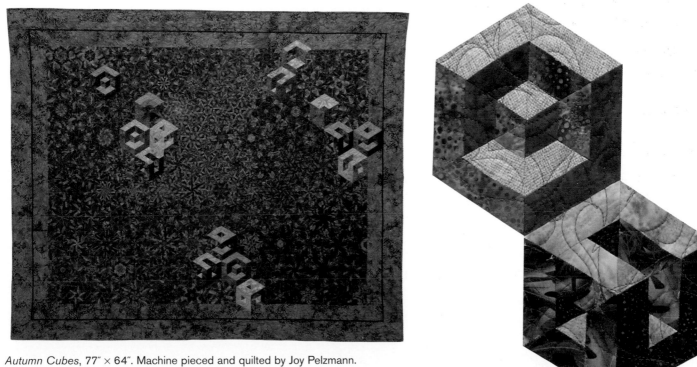

Autumn Cubes, 77″ × 64″. Machine pieced and quilted by Joy Pelzmann.

Anni's Quilt, 71″ × 60″. Machine pieced and quilted by Maxine Rosenthal.

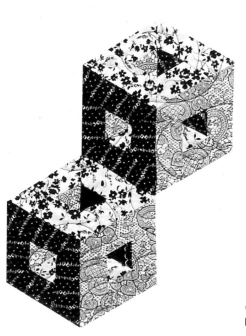

Operation Migration Second Raffle Quilt, 69″ × 60″. Machine pieced by Nancy Drew. Quilted by Lois Koester at Faye's Henhouse Quilts, Mayville, North Dakota.

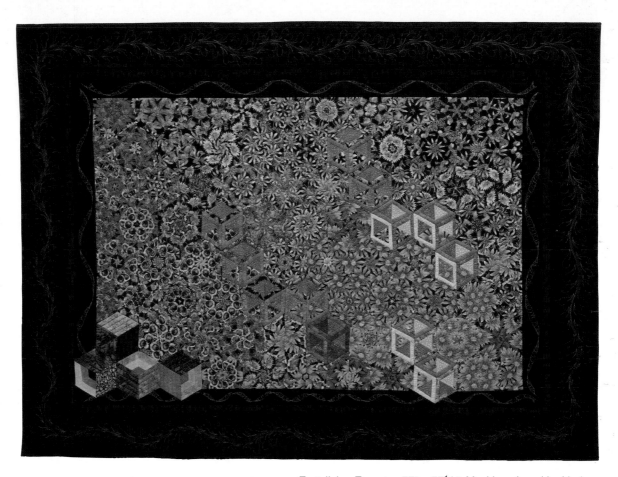

Swiss Chard, 56″ × 46″. Machine pieced and quilted by Maxine Rosenthal.

Tantalizing Tapestry, 77″ × 57½″. Machine pieced by Linda Vikla of Blue Bamboo. Quilted by Theresa Francisco. Linda says, "Over the years I have made countless projects in needlepoint, knitting, counted cross-stitch, and quilting. I have enjoyed everything, but my most favorite endeavors have involved working with Maxine's book. Now these are the only quilts I want to make. With Maxine's designs, I can make a one-of-a-kind work of art not just once but several times over."

Chickens in My Yard, 72″ × 64″. Machine pieced and quilted by Maxine Rosenthal.

Chapter 4
designing with multiple colorways of the same fabric

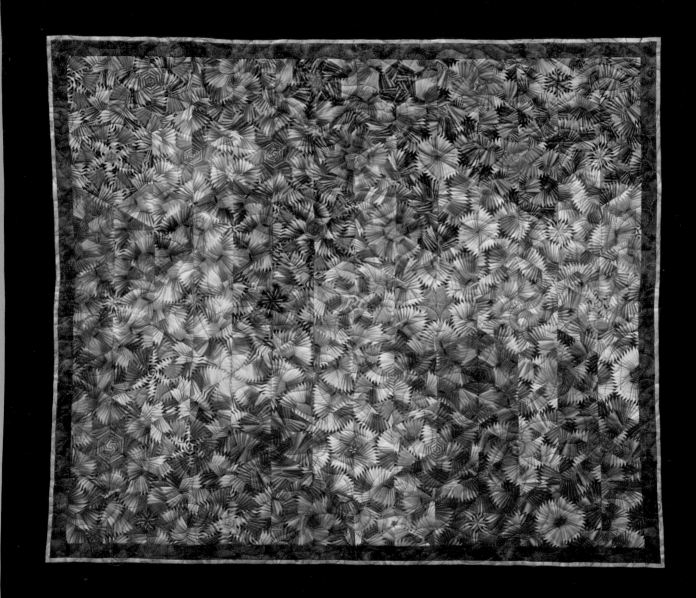

Ménage à Trois, 48″ × 41″. Machine pieced and quilted by Maxine Rosenthal.

ometimes we have a hard time deciding between multiple colorways while shopping for fabric. The next time this happens to you, think about buying several colorways to use in the same quilt. You can even share your extra fabric with a friend.

Choosing Fabric

For our example of working with multiple colorways of the same fabric, we chose a fabric with a 24˝ repeat and a large overall pattern. When some of the colors repeat across colorways, you automatically limit the palette. When the color palettes are very different they don't blend as well. Saturated color, strong design, and minimal background work best.

Selection of fabric

When working with two colorways, you need to have six identical repeats of both fabrics because you will be cutting and aligning twelve layers at the same time. This process creates identical triangles and allows you to easily exchange triangles within a block. You will not be losing any blocks but creating a second mirror block in the other colorway.

If you are buying with a friend, you can each have three strips of all twelve layers after the strips are cut. This is enough for 108–114 blocks.

Prepare the fabric as you did when you were working with six layers. Align all the layers at the same time. Be sure to put a new blade in your rotary cutter—cutting twelve layers with an old blade is no fun.

Alignment of twelve layers

Now you are ready to sew your blocks. This design approach requires some unsewing but is well worth it for the added impact. Just consider it part of the design process! Choose the colorway that you want to predominate the quilt. Sew one stack of six triangles into half hexagons and pin the halves together. Pin the six triangles of the other colorway to the back of each pinned hexagon. Pinning keeps together all those triangles you carefully cut at the same time. Repeat the process for each stack of triangles.

Designing

Now you're ready to begin designing with the blocks made from the dominant colorway.

1. Arrange the hexagon blocks around the edge of the design wall. If you are working with blocks from just three strips, you'll have plenty of space to spread out.

Blocks around edge of design wall

2. Arrange these blocks in a design that is pleasing to you. Remember that the triangles in the other colorway are still pinned to the back of each block.

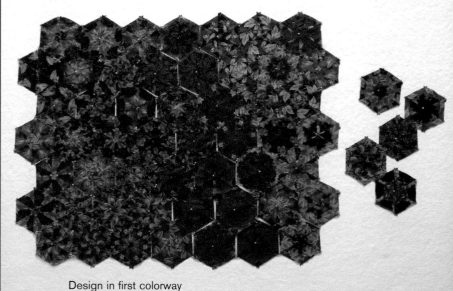

Design in first colorway

3. Pin each block to the design wall. You will be jostling these blocks as you dig for triangles of the other colorway and you don't want to alter your arrangement. Now form a secondary design by replacing triangles in various hexagons. This process will both create an additional pattern and smooth out odd transitions between blocks. *As you pin a triangle over the original kaleidoscope hexagon, remember to keep the straight of grain to the outside of the block.* If you do this, the kaleidoscope will be exact, with just a shift in color. This shift in color creates excitement and movement all by itself.

Redesign using triangles from second colorway

4. Change as many blocks as you want. Here is another example based on the same first colorway design. Adding triangles from the second colorway forms a bolder design.

Second design with triangles from both colorways

5. Periodically stand back to get the total effect. Changing adjacent triangles of two separate hexagons forms a new shape.

6. Once you have determined your final design, unstitch and re-sew the "new" half hexagons. Keep the triangles you have taken out of the first colorway with the second colorway triangles so you can use them in another quilt. They too will form a complete hexagon, possibly a mirror image of the first.

Form large triangle by replacing parts of two hexagons.

One-of-a-Kind Quilt with Two Colorways of the Same Fabric

Sharing DNA, 73″ × 48″. Machine pieced and quilted by Maxine Rosenthal.

Original fabrics

Materials

4½ yards each of a large-scale print in 2 colorways (6 repeats plus ½ yard to include in the backing)

Inner-border fabric: ½ yard

Accent-border fabric: ¼ yard

Outer-border and binding fabric: 1⅔ yards

Backing: 2½ yards*

Batting: 77″ × 52″

*This quantity assumes you will include ½ yard of the original fabric in the backing.

⬡ ⬡ ⬡

BEFORE YOU BEGIN: Refer to *Creating Hexagons*, page 10, for details on cutting repeats, aligning fabrics, cutting triangles, and sewing half hexagons.

Cutting

Block Fabrics

1. Divide the 2 fabrics into 12 identical repeats, 6 of each colorway.

2. Align all 12 layers exactly.

3. Trim one edge of the 12 layers and cut a minimum of 4 strips 3¾″ × the width of the fabric. This is enough to make at least 72 blocks. We used 70 blocks total in the quilt shown.

4. Using the Clearview Triangle ruler, cut 3¾″ triangles through all 12 layers. Keep the triangles stacked together.

Border and Binding Fabrics

1. For the inner border, cut 6 strips 2½″ × the width of the fabric.

2. For the accent border, cut 6 strips ¾″ × the width of the fabric.

3. For the outer border, cut 6 strips 4½″ × the width of the fabric.

4. For the binding, cut 7 strips 2½″ × the width of the fabric.

Sewing and Design

1. Choose the colorway you want to be dominant.

2. Sew the triangles into half hexagons, pressing the seams open. Pin the halves together. Also pin the triangles of the secondary colorway to the corresponding block in the dominant colorway. Keep all matching triangles together throughout the sewing and pressing process to minimize errors and make your life easier.

3. Place the blocks of the primary colorway on the design wall, beginning with 7 horizontal rows of 10 blocks each, leaving the extra triangles pinned to the back. Create an arrangement that you like, filling in the sides with half blocks as needed.

4. Remove the pinned triangles from the backs of the blocks and place the triangles on top wherever you think they look good. You are free to add blocks that are composed entirely of the second colorway, as well as mirrors of the blocks composed of both colorways, to complete this quilt. Horizontal rows of 10 blocks each were used.

5. Re-sew the modified hexagons and return them to the wall.

6. Assemble the quilt top in vertical rows.

7. Square off the top and bottom edges.

Finishing

1. Measure your quilt vertically through the center. Use this measurement to cut 2 strips of the inner-border fabric, piecing as needed. Sew a strip to each side of the quilt.

2. Measure your quilt horizontally through the center, including the borders just added. Use this measurement to cut 2 strips of inner-border fabric to the measured length, piecing as necessary, and sew the strips to the top and bottom of the quilt.

3. Repeat the measuring process to add the accent border and outer border to the quilt.

4. Make a backing. Quilt and bind.

Chapter 5
designing with two fabrics of the same colorway

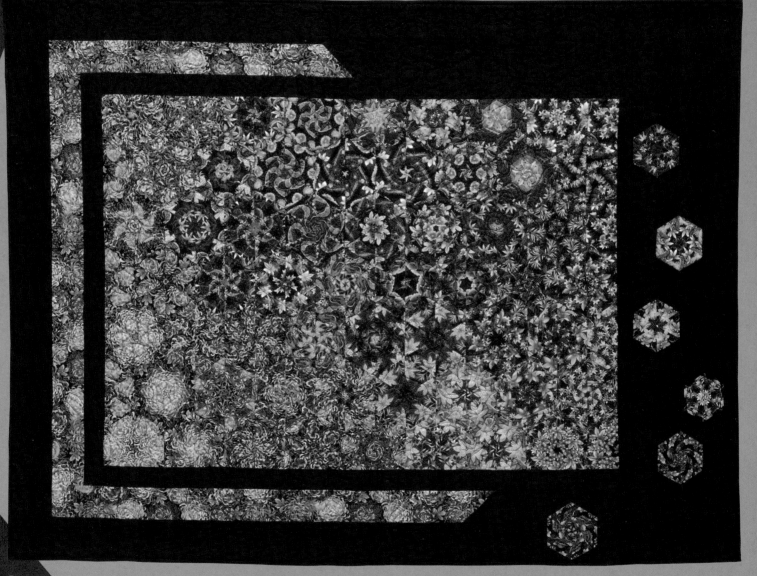

Dragons in the Garden, 68″ × 52″. Machine pieced and quilted by Joy Pelzmann.

When you look at a landscape, you'll see that variation in scale adds interest to nature's composition. Using two fabrics of the same colorway but in different scales recreates this complexity in your quilt without increasing the difficulty of sewing. Fabric manufacturers kindly provide companion fabrics, so all you have to do is shop.

Choosing Fabric

When searching for fabric, look at the color dots along the selvages. If two fabrics share a number of color dots, the fabrics may work together, but it's better to stick with fabrics from a single collection from a given manufacturer. We tend to pick fabrics that have strong designs with almost no background. Using fabrics of this type makes the difference in scale more striking.

These are the fabrics we began with.

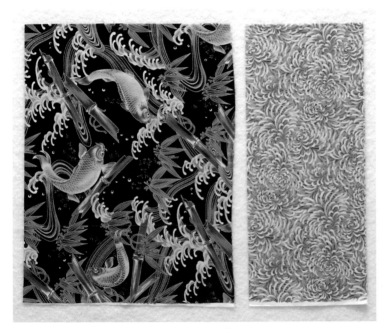

Selection of fabric

How Much Fabric to Buy?

You still need six repeats of each fabric. You'll require a full 5 yards of the primary fabric, probably the larger repeat (24˝). The secondary, smaller print will have a shorter repeat, but you still need six repeats. This is another opportunity to shop with a friend and share.

Designing

Start by putting all hexagons made from the primary fabric on your design wall. Create a pattern you find pleasing. Remember that you will be modifying this pattern as you add hexagons from the secondary fabric, so leave spaces here and there to fit them in.

Initial design

When adding the secondary kaleidoscopes, you can replace either whole blocks or just parts of blocks. We never mind unsewing for design purposes. As you will notice in this example, the colors are perfectly coordinated, but the secondary fabric is quite light. We played off this duality of light and dark and created the quilt design shown; we called it *Out of the Darkness, Into the Light*. Had the values been equal, we might have chosen a very different design.

Design with light and dark fabrics

One-of-a-Kind Quilt with
Two Fabrics of the Same Colorway

Friends at Play, 68″ × 49″. Machine pieced by Maxine Rosenthal and Joy Pelzmann. Quilted by Maxine Rosenthal.

Original fabric

Materials

4½ yards each of 2 companion fabrics (6 repeats plus ½ yard to include in the backing)

Border and binding fabric: 2¼ yards

Accent-border fabric: ¼ yard

Backing: 2¾ yards*

Batting: 72″ × 53″

*This quantity assumes you will include ½ yard of the original fabric in the backing.

● ⬢ ◆

Before you begin: Refer to *Creating Hexagons*, page 10, for details on cutting repeats, aligning fabrics, cutting triangles, and sewing half hexagons.

Cutting

Block Fabrics

1. Choose the fabric you want to be dominant. Divide the 2 fabrics into 12 repeats, 6 of each companion fabric.

2. Align each set of 6 layers exactly.

3. Trim one edge of each set of 6. From the primary fabric, cut 4 strips 3¾″ × the width of the fabric. From the secondary fabric, cut 3 strips 3¾″ × the width of the fabric. This is enough to make 72 blocks of the primary fabric and 54 blocks of the secondary fabric. We used about 72 blocks total in the quilt shown.

4. Using the Clearview Triangle ruler, cut 3¾″ triangles through all 6 layers. Keep the triangles stacked together.

Border and Binding Fabrics

1. For the borders, cut:

2 strips 4¾″ × the width of the fabric

4 strips 3¾″ × the width of the fabric

5 strips 3″ × the width of the fabric

2 strips 2½″ × the width of the fabric

3 strips 1½″ × the width of the fabric

2 strips ¾″ × the width of the fabric

1 square 5¾″ × 5¾″

2. For the accent border, cut 2 strips ¾″ × the width of the fabric.

3. For the binding, cut 7 strips 2½″ × the width of the fabric.

Sewing and Design

1. Sew the triangles into half hexagons, pressing the seams open. Pin the halves together. Do this for both fabrics.

2. Place the blocks on the design wall and create a pleasing design using the hexagons from the primary fabric first.

3. Add hexagons from the secondary fabric. You can simply add just 1 triangle from a block, half a block, or any combination of triangles. To make a quilt approximately the same size as ours, arrange the blocks in 8 horizontal rows of 9 blocks each. Fill the sides with half blocks.

4. Re-sew any modified half hexagons and put them back on the design wall. Take away 4 blocks from the left half of the bottom row.

5. Assemble the quilt top in vertical rows, separating it into 2 sections, breaking it where you removed the lower blocks.

Section 1 Section 2

 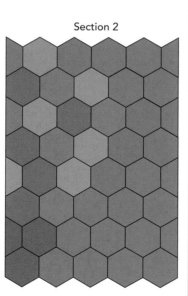

6. Square off the top and bottom edges of each section.

7. Measure over 3″ along the bottom from the lower left corner of section 2. From here, cut off the corner at a 60° angle to the bottom edge.

Section 2

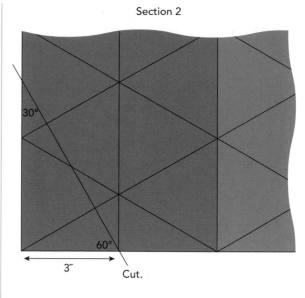

8. Using the 5¾″ square of border fabric, cut one end at a 60° angle and sew the cut square to section 2. Trim even with the vertical edge.

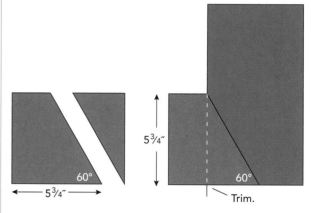

9. Sew together 3 of the extra hexagon blocks and trim them into squares 4¾″ × 4¾″ for the border by placing the 2⅜″ mark of a square ruler on the center of the block. Trim 2 sides; then rotate the ruler and trim the other 2 sides. Center the ruler wherever you think the trimmed block will look best.

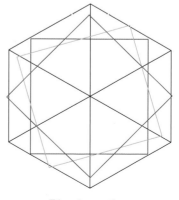

Trimming options

10. Measure the width of section 1; subtract $4\frac{1}{4}$″ from this measurement and cut a $4\frac{3}{4}$″ border strip to that length. Cut a $1\frac{1}{2}$″ border strip to the original full width measurement.

11. Sew a squared-off block to the end of the $4\frac{3}{4}$″ border strip from Step 10 and then add the $1\frac{1}{2}$″ strip to the top.

12. Sew the border unit from Step 11 to the bottom of section 1. Sew section 1 to section 2.

13. Measure your quilt through the center vertically and add a $1\frac{1}{2}$″ border to the left side and a 3″ border to the right side.

14. Sew the remaining 2 squared-off blocks together with a $1\frac{1}{2}$″ × $4\frac{3}{4}$″ rectangle; then add a $4\frac{3}{4}$″-wide strip to the top block. Trim this unit to the correct length and add this to the left side of the quilt.

15. Measure horizontally through the center of the quilt and add a 3″ border to the top.

16. For the accent border, attach a $\frac{3}{4}$″ strip of the border fabric to the $\frac{3}{4}$″ strip of accent-border fabric at a 45° angle, as shown. Make 2 strips, one for the top and one for the right side. Play with these strips on the design wall until you are satisfied with the placement. Trim as needed and add them to the right side and top of the quilt.

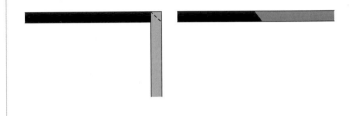

17. Measure the quilt as before to add a $3\frac{3}{4}$″ border to the right side and then to the top.

18. Measure the quilt and add a $2\frac{1}{2}$″ border strip to the left side and then a 3″ strip to the bottom.

19. Make a backing. Quilt and bind.

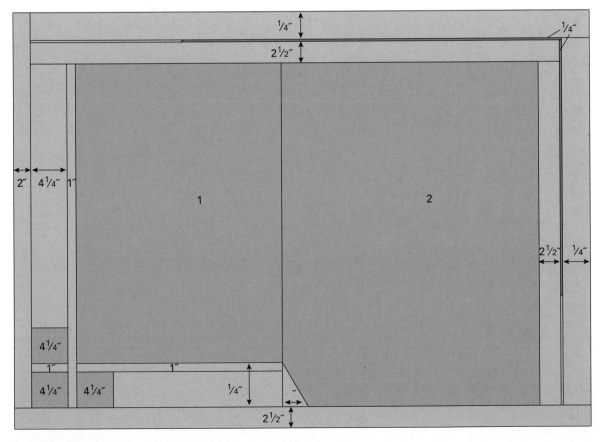

Assembly diagram

Asian Surprise, 56¹/₂″ × 49″. Machine pieced and quilted by Kristen Bender. Kristen says, "I made this quilt using two fabrics from the Suzuko Collection by Kona Bay. It was really fun to make and exciting to see how the blocks would turn out. It's hard to believe you can get so much variety from a single fabric. When I have shown this quilt to family and friends, they can't believe I used only two fabrics. The effect is amazing!"

creating a quilt with panels

Chinese Take Out, 33″ × 56″. Machine pieced and quilted by Joy Pelzmann.

There are several reasons for creating a quilt with panels. Creating panels allows you to play with geometry. Your border fabrics also become integral to the design; the border moves through the quilt, not just around it.

Sometimes even though the fabric is lovely and the blocks are beautiful, the quilt top just doesn't seem to come together. Maybe you don't want a rectangular quilt. Let's not forget that special-occasion queen-size bed quilt: perfect fabric, gorgeous blocks, but you bought only 5 yards of fabric. Oops! Here come panels to the rescue.

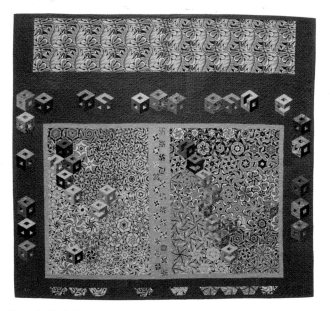

Petra's Quilt, 94″ × 89″. Machine pieced and quilted by Maxine Rosenthal.

Now it's time to play. Sometimes a random thought or image will come to you. Follow that lead—often it is the first step to your design solution. For example, the richly colored paisley pattern of the original fabric below reminded us of a kimono. This led us to design three panels that suggest the body and the sleeves of a kimono.

Original fabric

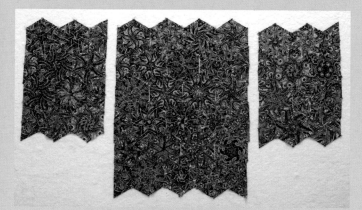

Panels to reflect kimono design

Once you've established the basic form, strengthen the image through the spacing and placement of borders. The selection of border fabrics can enhance this impression.

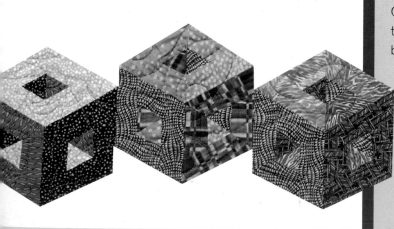

One-of-a-Kind Quilt Made with Panels

Maid in Japan, 97″ × 61$\frac{1}{2}$″. Machine pieced and quilted by Joy Pelzmann.

Original fabric

Materials

$4\frac{1}{2}$ yards of fabric for hexagon blocks (6 repeats plus $\frac{1}{2}$ yard to include in the backing)

Black border and binding fabric: 3 yards

Red accent-border fabric: $\frac{3}{4}$ yard

Backing: $5\frac{1}{2}$ yards*

Batting: $103˝ \times 68˝$

*This quantity assumes you will include $\frac{1}{2}$ yard of the original fabric in the backing.

● ◆ ⬡

Before you begin: Refer to *Creating Hexagons*, page 10, for details on cutting repeats, aligning fabrics, cutting triangles, and sewing half hexagons.

Cutting

Block Fabric

1. Divide the fabric into 6 identical repeats.

2. Align all 6 layers exactly.

3. Trim one edge of the 6 layers and cut 6 strips $3\frac{3}{4}˝ \times$ the width of the fabric.

4. Using the Clearview Triangle ruler, cut $3\frac{3}{4}˝$ triangles through all 6 layers. Cut as many triangles as possible from all the strips. Keep the triangles stacked together.

Border and Binding Fabrics

1. For the black borders, cut:

   8 strips $4\frac{1}{2}˝ \times$ the width of the fabric

   1 strip $3\frac{3}{4}˝ \times$ the width of the fabric; from this strip, cut 3 triangles using the Clearview Triangle ruler. Cut more if needed for your design.

   1 strip $3\frac{1}{2}˝ \times$ the width of the fabric

   1 strip $3\frac{1}{4}˝ \times$ the width of the fabric

   8 strips $2\frac{1}{2}˝ \times$ the width of the fabric

   3 strips $2˝ \times$ the width of the fabric

2. For the red accent border, cut:

   11 strips $\frac{3}{4}˝ \times$ the width of the fabric

   6 strips $2˝ \times$ the width of the fabric

3. For the binding, cut 9 strips $2\frac{1}{2}˝ \times$ the width of the fabric.

Sewing and Design

1. Sew the triangles into half hexagons, pressing the seams open. Pin the halves together. You will need 114 blocks to make the quilt as shown.

2. The design is made of 3 panels. Place blocks on the design wall as follows: the left panel is made of 9 rows of $5\frac{1}{2}$ blocks; the center panel is made of 9 rows of 4 blocks; the right panel is made of 9 rows of 3 blocks and has an uneven edge.

3. Assemble the left and center panels by sewing the half hexagons together in vertical rows.

4. For the right panel, which has uneven edges, sew a half hexagon using the 3 triangles cut from the black fabric to fill in the edge as needed. Sew the half hexagons together in 6 vertical rows.

5. To create the uneven border on the right panel, make a strip set by sewing a $\frac{3}{4}˝$ accent-border strip to the $3\frac{1}{4}˝$ black border strip. Referring to *Hexagons or Cubes Falling Out of the Quilt*, page 68, make a vertical row of half hexagons and border fabric, using the strip set and the $3\frac{1}{2}˝$ strip of black border fabric. Cut the border strips at a 60° angle to join them to the half hexagon blocks. Sew this strip to the remainder of the panel to create a rectangle.

6. Sew together the remaining ³/₄″ red strips to form a long strip and use these strips to add borders to the left and center panels and the remaining 3 sides of the right panel. Measure each panel vertically through the center. Use this measurement to cut 2 strips of the accent-border fabric. Sew a border strip to the sides of each panel.

7. Measure the panels horizontally through the center, including the borders just added. Cut strips of accent-border fabric to the measured length and attach them to the top and bottom of the panels. For the top of the right panel, you will need to add a piece of black to the red accent border. Cut a ³/₄″ × 3¹/₂″ piece of black fabric and sew it to the red accent strip. Align the seam with the seam of the red accent piece below.

8. Sew 2¹/₂″ border strips together to form 1 long strip and use this strip to join the 3 panels together.

9. Add the remainder of the 2¹/₂″ strip to the top, bottom, and left sides, measuring through the center as before.

10. Sew the 2″ red strips together to form a long strip.

11. Measure and attach a 2″ red border to the left side of the quilt top.

12. Sew a 2″ black strip to the remaining red strip at a 45° angle. Audition this strip unit to decide where you want the change of color to fall. Cut the strip and add it to the top of the quilt. Repeat for the bottom.

13. Measure the quilt vertically through the center. Add a 2″ black border to the right side of the quilt.

14. Measure the quilt and use the 4¹/₂″ black strips to add the outermost border on all sides.

15. Make a backing. Quilt and bind.

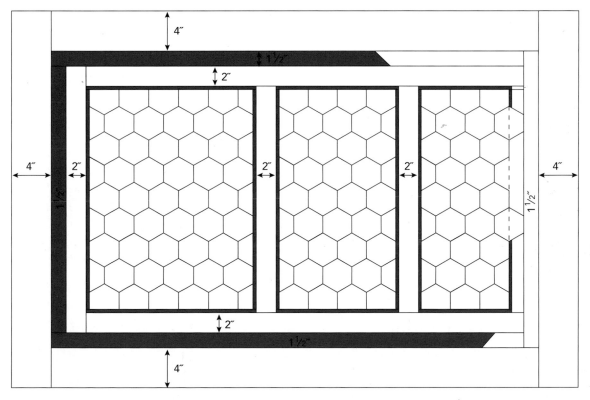

Assembly diagram

Chapter 7
dividing a quilt asymmetrically

Along the Beltway, 68″ × 69½″. Machine pieced and quilted by Joy Pelzmann.

Nothing makes an impact like breaking up a design in an unexpected way. This process takes advantage of the angles created by a hexagon and magnifies their impact. The hard edges created make this a very clean design, great for a modern home or an office setting.

Sometimes you will begin a quilt knowing you will divide it asymmetrically. On other occasions, you'll find that the overall pattern just needs something more, and you will choose this dramatic approach. Either way, begin with an overall design. Note the extra blocks along the side. We don't always use every block that we make.

Overall design

Put the blocks on the wall with the unsewn seams running vertically. The photograph shows a smaller group of blocks with the seams open and apart for clarity, but your half hexagons should still be butted together. The photographs show the process with just a few blocks. Use this technique with any number of blocks.

Place unsewn seams vertically.

Stand back from your piece and ask yourself, "What if? What if I break it at this angle? What if I pull out a large triangle?" The options are endless. Once you have decided on the angle, rotate the individual blocks so the open seams align with and create the chosen angle. The photograph shows the same group of blocks that have been rotated to create the desired angle.

Realign blocks.

As you can see, whole blocks rotate easily, but half blocks at the ends of rows may need to be divided again. Use a seam ripper to separate triangles as necessary.

Divide side blocks.

When you assemble the rows, note that they are on the diagonal, not on the vertical. It's easy to assemble and gives your quilt a whole new look.

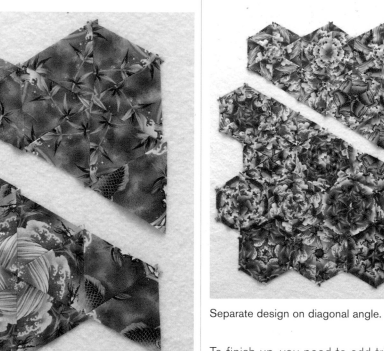

Assemble blocks in diagonal rows.

Because the orientation has been changed, creating a new design by separating the layout along an open seam is easy.

Separate design on diagonal angle.

To finish up, you need to add triangles here and there and take away half hexagons to create straight sides.

Add triangles to fill in.

One-of-a-Kind Quilt Divided Asymmetrically

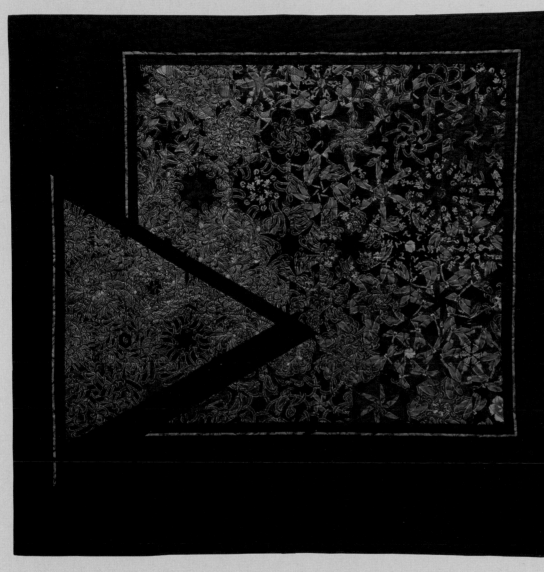

Breaking out of the Mold, 55$\frac{1}{2}$″ × 54$\frac{1}{2}$″. Machine pieced and quilted by Maxine Rosenthal.

Original fabric

Materials

$4\frac{1}{2}$ yards of fabric for hexagon blocks (6 repeats plus $\frac{1}{2}$ yard to include in the backing)

Dark border and binding fabric: $2\frac{5}{8}$ yards

Accent-border fabric: $\frac{1}{4}$ yard

Backing: 3 yards*

Batting: 57″ × 58″

*This quantity assumes you will include $\frac{1}{2}$ yard of the original fabric in the backing.

◆　⬡　⬡

Before you begin: Refer to *Creating Hexagons*, page 10, for details on cutting repeats, aligning fabrics, cutting triangles, and sewing half hexagons.

Cutting

Block Fabric

1. Divide the fabric into 6 identical repeats.

2. Align all 6 layers exactly.

3. Trim one edge of the 6 layers and cut 4 strips $3\frac{3}{4}$″ × the width of the fabric. This is enough to make 72–76 blocks. Cut 1 or 2 more strips if you want to make more blocks. We used approximately 60 blocks total in the quilt shown but we used all the blocks to begin the initial design.

4. Using the Clearview Triangle ruler, cut $3\frac{3}{4}$″ triangles through all 6 layers. Keep the triangles stacked together.

Border and Binding Fabrics

1. For the dark borders, cut:

　　5 strips 2″ × the width of the fabric

　　1 strip $3\frac{1}{2}$″ × the width of the fabric

　　1 strip $1\frac{1}{2}$″ × the width of the fabric

　　1 strip 5″ × the width of the fabric

　　3 strips 4″ × the width of the fabric

　　3 strips $12\frac{1}{2}$″ × the width of the fabric

2. For the accent border, cut 6 strips $\frac{3}{4}$″ × the width of the fabric.

3. For the binding, cut 6 strips $2\frac{1}{2}$″ × the width of the fabric.

Sewing and Design

1. Sew the triangles into half hexagons, pressing the seams open. Pin the halves together.

2. Begin by designing a typical quilt center, placing blocks on the design wall in 7 horizontal rows of 6 blocks each. Align all hexagons so the pinned seamline is at an angle. Add half blocks along the left and right edges to fill in.

3. Once you are pleased with the overall design, count down 3 complete rows along the left edge and begin moving hexagons to the left to create a large triangle unit, separating half hexagons as needed.

4. Sew the half blocks together in diagonal rows to create the large triangle unit.

5. Sew the remaining hexagons together into 2 sections, creating a break where the diagonal line continues from the separated triangle. Then trim the top and bottom edges straight.

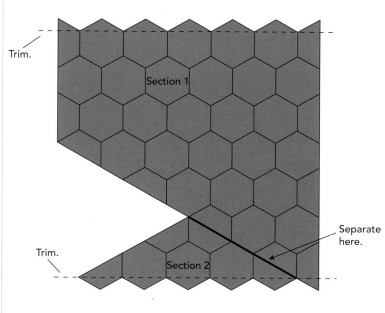

6. Sew a strip of border fabric 2″ wide to the top edge of the triangle unit. Trim the corners even with the triangle edges, as shown (this is a 60° angle).

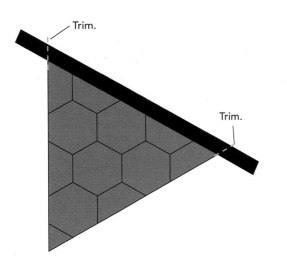

Trim.

Trim.

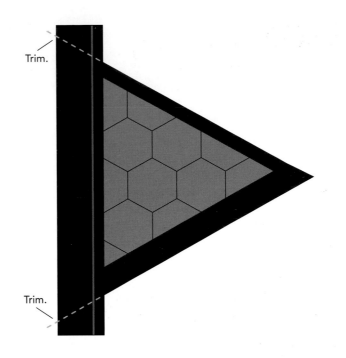

Trim.

Trim.

7. Sew a strip of border fabric 3$\frac{1}{2}$″ wide to the bottom edge of the triangle unit. Trim the corners as before. You will need to maintain that 60° angle on your borders.

9. Sew sections 1 and 2 together for 8″ to 10″ at the lower right corner, creating a partial seam. This process will allow you to easily add borders to the bottom and side.

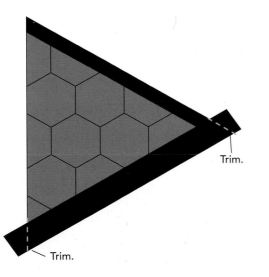

Trim.

Trim.

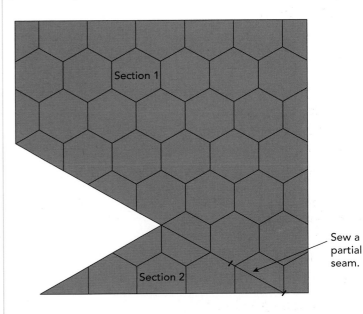

Section 1

Section 2

Sew a partial seam.

8. Sew together a strip of border fabric 1$\frac{1}{2}$″ wide, an accent-border strip $\frac{3}{4}$″ wide, and a border strip 5″ wide. Sew this strip set to the vertical edge of the triangle unit, having the widest strip of border fabric to the outside, and centering the strip set on the triangle. This placement will give you plenty of fabric for cutting the corners at a 60° angle. Trim the ends.

10. Measure the length and width of the quilt and add 2″-wide strips of border fabric to the 4 sides of the center quilt section. Do not worry about the open triangular section right now.

11. Measure again and add ³/₄″-wide strips of accent-border fabric to the 4 sides of the quilt center. Trim the left edge at a 60° angle to align with section 1. Trim the bottom edge at a 30° angle to align with section 2.

12. Sew 4″ strips of border fabric to the top and right side of the quilt.

13. Piece 2 strips of border fabric 12¹/₂″ wide and sew them to the bottom of the quilt, letting the excess extend at the left edge; trim the excess at an angle to align with section 2.

Add the remaining 12¹/₂″ strip to the left side of the quilt center and trim the lower edge to a 60° angle to align with section 1.

14. Sew the triangle unit to the main body of the quilt along the lower edge. Then sew it to the main body of the quilt along the upper edge, completing the diagonal seam.

15. Trim any uneven edges and square up the corners of the quilt.

16. Make a backing. Quilt and bind.

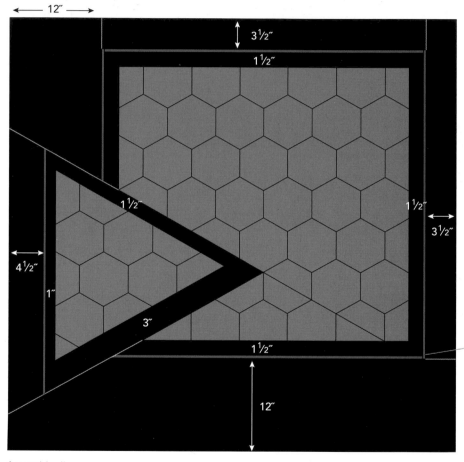

Assembly diagram

Chapter 8
replacing triangles

Triangles Gone Wild, 64″ × 58″. Machine pieced by Maxine Rosenthal and Joy Pelzmann. Quilted by Maxine Rosenthal.

ometimes your lovely fabric makes interesting kaleidoscopes, but the overall design of the quilt lacks wow. At other times, you love the play of the hexagons, but there are spots where the transition from one block to the next just doesn't work. Here is a way to solve these problems and add energy and motion to your quilt.

Adding Additional Design to Your Quilt

Your initial design is complete, yet you yearn for something more.

Initial design

Secondary design

Stand back and consider a secondary design. Select a fabric or several fabrics that work well with your quilt. Cut 3³/₄″ strips of these fabrics and then cut triangles from the strips. Now play with these—you have absolute freedom to experiment because you are merely placing them on top of existing hexagons. The final shape will develop as you work.

Arranging triangles around a hexagon can easily suggest a flower or a sun.

The possibilities are endless.

Arrange the triangles in a directional manner to change the viewer's focus.

Moving the eye through the quilt

Transitions for Those Awkward Moments

You have arranged and rearranged kaleidoscopes, and everything is just about perfect except in one or two places. Triangles are great for these places. When you put a triangle in place of a difficult transition, the viewer no longer notices the transition. Then you can add a few more triangles to create a secondary design.

Triangle at an awkward transition

Replacing several triangles

You can also add a few triangles in the border to extend and unify the design, as in the quilt below. (Refer to *Adding Triangles to the Border*, page 70.)

Forever Sunshine, 42″ × 40″. Machine pieced and quilted by Joy Pelzmann.

Triangles Made from Two Fabrics

You can add even more interest if you cut your triangles from a strip set pieced of two fabrics. One of the strips could be the primary fabric if you like.

Add pieced triangles made from two fabrics.

One-of-a-Kind Quilt Using Triangles

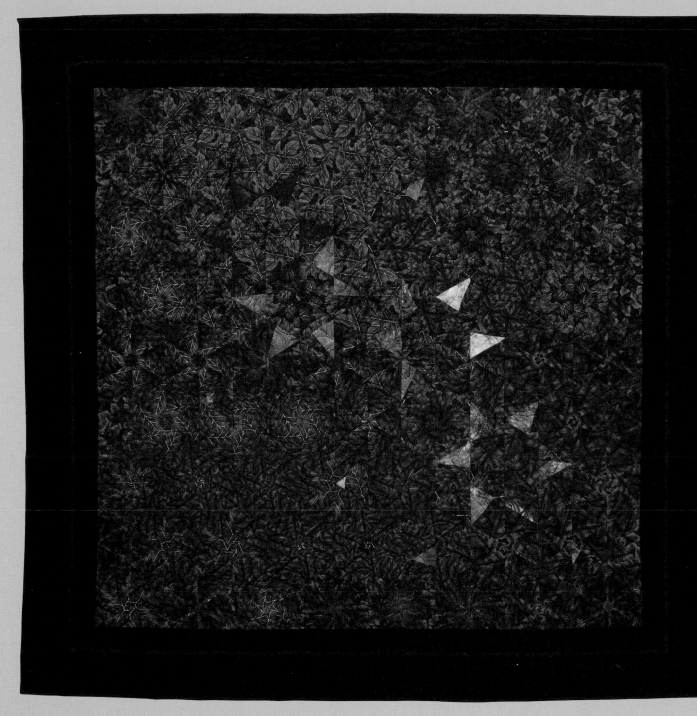

Midnight Flowers, 61″ × 58¹/₂″. Machine pieced and quilted by Joy Pelzmann.

Materials

4$\frac{1}{2}$ yards of fabric for hexagon blocks (6 repeats plus $\frac{1}{2}$ yard to include in the backing)

One or more fat quarters of coordinating fabrics for triangles

Border and binding fabric: 2$\frac{1}{4}$ yards

Accent-border fabric: $\frac{1}{4}$ yard

Backing: 3 yards*

Batting: 65″ × 63″

*This quantity assumes you will include $\frac{1}{2}$ yard of the original fabric in the backing.

◆ ● ◆

Before you begin: Refer to *Creating Hexagons*, page 10, for details on cutting repeats, aligning fabrics, cutting triangles, and sewing half hexagons.

Cutting

Block Fabric

1. Divide the fabric into 6 identical repeats.

2. Align all 6 layers exactly.

3. Trim one edge of the 6 layers and cut 6 strips 3$\frac{3}{4}$″ × the width of the fabric.

4. Using the Clearview Triangle ruler, cut 3$\frac{3}{4}$″ triangles through all 6 layers. Keep the triangles stacked together.

Border and Binding Fabrics

1. For the inner border, cut 5 strips 2$\frac{1}{2}$″ × the width of the fabric.

2. For the accent border, cut 6 strips $\frac{3}{4}$″ × the width of the fabric.

3. For the outer border, cut 6 strips 4$\frac{1}{2}$″ × the width of the fabric.

4. For the binding, cut 6 strips 2$\frac{1}{2}$″ × the width of the fabric.

Sewing and Design

1. Sew the triangles into half hexagons, pressing the seams open. Pin the halves together. You will need 72 blocks to make the quilt as shown.

2. Place the blocks on the design wall, beginning with 9 horizontal rows of 8 blocks each. Rearrange the blocks, filling in the sides with half blocks, until you have a pleasing initial design.

3. Cut triangles from 3$\frac{3}{4}$″ strips of the coordinating fabrics—these can be cut either from a single fabric or from pieced strips. Pieced strips offer another opportunity for creativity. They result in a more complex triangle. If you use one of your primary fabrics in the strip set, as we did, the triangles of the other fabric will appear narrower, or smaller in the quilt, because the primary fabric will blend in.

4. Add triangles to the overall design, re-sewing half hexagons as needed.

5. Assemble the quilt top by sewing together the vertical rows.

6. Square off the top and bottom edges.

Finishing

1. Measure your quilt vertically through the center. Use this measurement to cut 2 strips of the inner-border fabric, piecing as needed. Sew a strip to each side of the quilt.

2. Measure your quilt horizontally through the center, including the borders just added. Use this measurement to cut 2 strips of inner-border fabric to the measured length, piecing as necessary, and sew the strips to the top and bottom of the quilt.

3. Repeat the measuring process to add the accent border and the outer border to the quilt.

4. Make a backing. Quilt and bind.

Chapter 9
borders

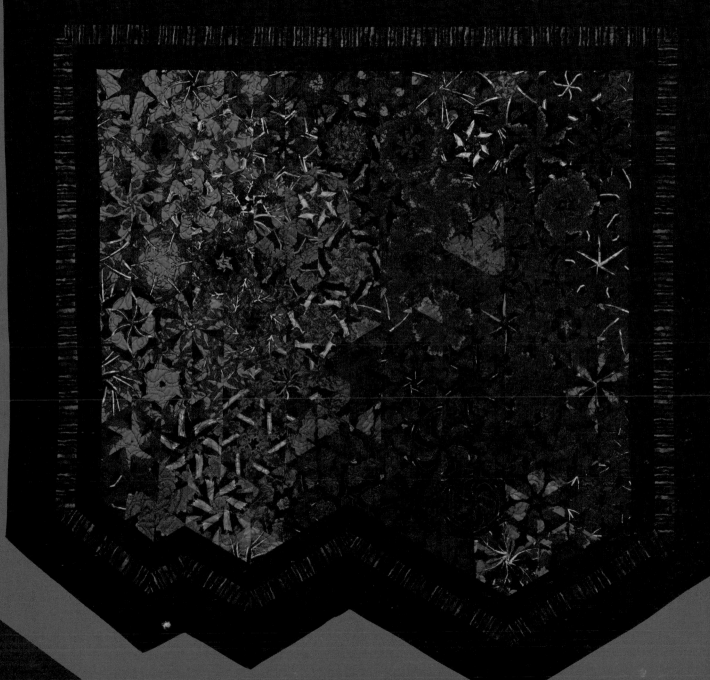

Study in Red and Brown, 56″ × 56″. Machine pieced and quilted by Joy Pelzmann.

Our trademark should be "Looks hard but is easy." In this chapter, we offer a series of suggestions for borders, starting with the most traditional and moving to something more complex. Once your kaleidoscopes have been assembled and enhanced with coordinating fabrics and shapes, a few additions to the border will raise your quilt to the next level. Remember, too, that borders don't always have to be the same width all around. Simply varying the width can add a spark to your design.

Some of the following techniques involve a number of steps, but each step is simple. You decide whether or not to use one technique or combine several in your quilt.

Adding Extra Kaleidoscopes to the Border

No doubt you have extra hexagons after assembling the main body of your quilt. The border is the perfect place to use them. Audition extra kaleidoscopes around the finished quilt. They not only add interest but also guide the viewer's eye.

The border fabric should be a solid color or a fabric that reads as a solid. The border will be pieced, and a solid color will hide the seams.

Audition kaleidoscopes for border.

1. Add a strip of border fabric to the quilt first; this initial strip stabilizes the quilt. Remember that there are many bias edges in these blocks, so measure the length of the quilt through the center to find the exact measurement for the inner border. We generally use a $2\frac{1}{2}$″-wide strip for the inner border, but the width is up to you.

2. At this point, the kaleidoscopes in the border are still pinned together as halves. Cut a strip of border fabric 3³⁄₄″ wide. Cut 3³⁄₄″ triangles using the Clearview Triangle ruler. Place a triangle between each half hexagon.

Add border triangles.

3. Sew the triangles to the half hexagons, creating 2 strips. Sew these strips together to create a middle border.

Sew half hexagons and triangles together.

4. If you do not want kaleidoscopes running the entire length of the border, trim the triangles, leaving ¹⁄₄″ beyond the hexagon point, and simply add a solid piece of the border fabric to complete the side. Remember that the border should be 6¹⁄₂″ wide to match the blocks.

Trim side triangles.

Add border fabric to extend border.

Hexagons or Cubes Falling Out of the Quilt

By allowing kaleidoscopes or cubes to move into the border, you increase the feeling of motion within the quilt. It is almost as if the design is too lively to be contained. You need to think this through before assembling the quilt.

Falling Out of the Side

When a half hexagon is an "extra piece," falling out into the border, keep it pinned until you are working on the first border strip. You are creating another vertical strip. These vertical border strips need to be cut at a 60° angle so they can be easily sewn to the half hexagon.

Adding border to half hexagon

Falling Out of the Bottom or Top

1. If a block is hanging out of the top or bottom, your quilt assembly process will have to be changed. First sew together all strips that are **not** falling out of the quilt.

Sew contained strips together.

2. In these completed sections, cut off the angled edges.

Cut off angled edges.

3. Cut a strip of border fabric 3½″ wide and cut a 60° angle at one end. Attach that 60° edge to the hanging half hexagons. Do this for all the hexagons that extend into the borders. Allow enough length for the border strips to extend a bit vertically beyond the horizontal borders that will be added.

Add strips to hanging hexagons.

4. Now sew the 2 block/border strips together. Add border strips to the remaining cut edges.

Add borders to remaining cut edges.

5. The outer border can be as wide as you want it to be. Now sew the 3 sections of the quilt together and trim the excess from the hanging hexagons to match the rest of the border. Add the side borders.

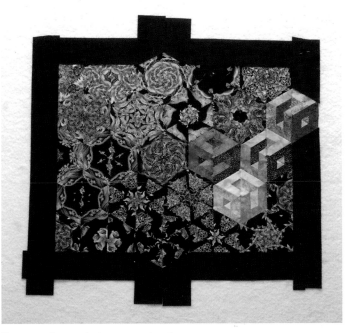

Sew together and trim excess borders.

Adding Triangles to the Border

Having designed a pleasing quilt, you may still be looking for something more. You may want to consider carrying an accent triangle into the border. Though the technique looks complicated, it is, as always, really easy.

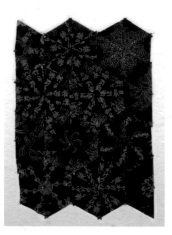

Initial design

1. Add a half hexagon of the accent fabric to the border area. Create a larger triangle that is half in and half out of the main body of the quilt by replacing the left center triangle of the adjacent half hexagon with a triangle cut from the accent fabric.

Add triangles to quilt center and border.

2. Sew the 3 border triangles together to create the half hexagon. Add a $3\frac{1}{2}$″-wide strip of the border fabric, cut at a 60° angle, to each end of the half hexagon, creating a rectangle.

Add border fabric to half hexagon.

3. Suspending a triangle in the border is also easy and effective. Attach a strip of border fabric to each side of the accent triangle in sequence, extending the border much further than you think you will need.

Add first border strip.

Add second border strip.

Add third border strip.

4. Then trim the unit into a square.

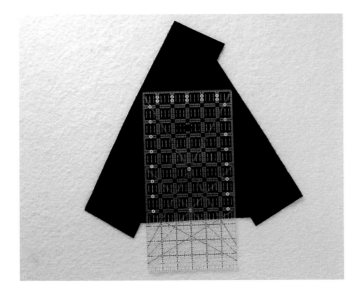

Either or both of these triangle options can be incorporated into the border. Enlarge the square or rectangle with additional border fabric as needed to equal the width of your border.

Banner Borders

Sometimes you will find that your initial design demands something other than straight borders. A banner border is a variation that works well with the hexagon blocks and triangle units.

Initial design

1. Remove half hexagons from the side edges.

Remove half hexagons from sides.

2. Add a hexagon to the bottom where you wish to create the lowest point of the banner. Again, the number of points is a personal decision; sometimes one point is enough, and other times you may want more.

Begin banner point.

3. Add extra half hexagons to fill in the point of the banner.

Add half hexagons.

4. Split these into 2 parts to allow easy assembly of vertical strips.

Split half hexagons.

5. Make adjustments to the rest of the half hexagons along the lower edge to create the angled line of your banner.

Adjust half hexagons to complete banner.

6. Sew the vertical strips together to the point of the banner, creating 2 halves.

Sew strips together.

7. The outside border will be added to each side of the banner and then mitered at the center. Begin by adding border fabric to both sides of the quilt and allow enough additional length (equivalent to the width of the border) at the bottom so you can miter the corner.

Add side borders.

8. Add the bottom border to the banner halves. Again, allow enough extra length on the outer sides. The center point of the banner is a 120° angle, which is two 60° angles. Cut one edge of each section of the bottom border into a 60° angle. Attach the bottom border to each section, allowing additional length to miter the outside edges where they meet the sides.

Add bottom borders; cut center ends at 60°.

9. Miter the outer corners and sew the 2 halves of the quilt together. Trim the top to a straight edge and attach the top border. Miter the corners and you are finished.

Complete the quilt top.

Three's Company, 42½″ × 42″.
Machine pieced and quilted by
Joy Pelzmann.

Midnight in the Garden of Eden,
66″ × 59″. Machine pieced and
quilted by Maxine Rosenthal.

One Whack Over the Line Sweet Mary, 41″ × 50″. Machine pieced and quilted by Maxine Rosenthal.

Encroachment, 68″ × 62″. Machine pieced and quilted by Maxine Rosenthal.

Hexagon Paradise, 58″ × 64″. Machine pieced and quilted by Debbie Manlove. Debbie says, "I loved making this quilt, from purchasing the fabric to putting on the binding. With help from my digital camera, the computer, and my friends, I got the color wash I wanted."

Fire and Ice, 44″ × 53″. Machine pieced and quilted by Joy Pelzmann.

Wisterious, 71¹/₂″ × 54″. Machine pieced by Elizabeth Vikla of Blue Bamboo. Quilted by Theresa Francisco. Elizabeth says, "I had sworn that I would never quilt, but I had to take those words back when I saw Maxine's first book, *One-Block Wonders*. Her simple technique made the process fun and easy to learn. Most people who see it can't believe that it's a first quilt."

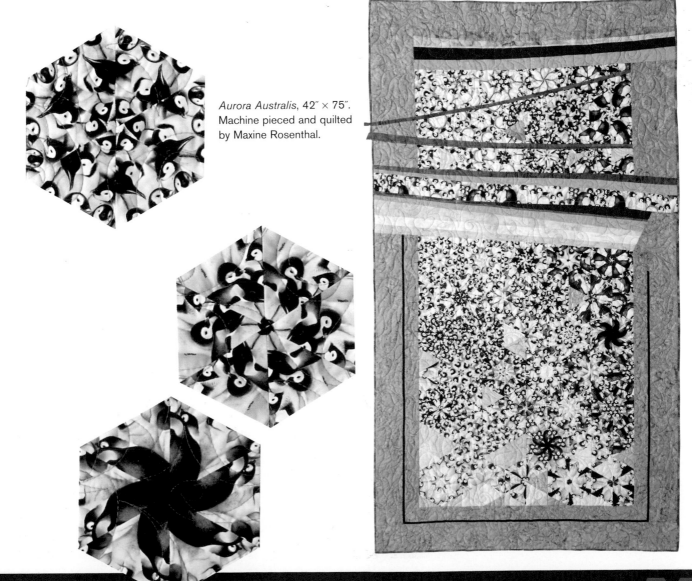

Aurora Australis, 42″ × 75″. Machine pieced and quilted by Maxine Rosenthal.

About
the authors

Photo by Joy Pelzmann

Maxine Rosenthal

Maxine Rosenthal wrote computer software before most people understood what a computer was. Those early days were a creative time, as programmers developed everything new to meet the needs of the user. Using a symbolic language to create a final product is not much different from using kaleidoscopes to create a quilt. Stretching the boundaries has not changed much for her. Playing with fabric, ideas, and a friend have been the rewards. That Maxine's daughter, an interior designer, is proud to use her mother's quilts in her home makes Maxine feel that the process needs to be shared with others.

Photo by Maxine Rosenthal

Joy Pelzmann

Joy Pelzmann has enjoyed a long and varied series of careers. Trained as a researcher in college, she went on to receive a Ph.D. in counseling psychology. Her academic career involved research, teaching, and training. Art and its application to the home arts have been lifelong interests. Now, finally, she is able to devote herself to those on a full-time basis. Immersed in her work as a quilt artist, she returns to teaching and training as a way of sharing her playful approach to art with others. A mother of three and grandmother of four, she sees life as a series of wonderful moments to be enjoyed and sometimes captured, but always appreciated.

Author Contact Info

Maxine Rosenthal
mjrosenth@msn.com

Joy Pelzmann
joypelz1@aol.com

Resources

For a list of other fine books from C&T Publishing, ask for a free catalog:

C&T Publishing, Inc.

P.O. Box 1456

Lafayette, CA 94549

(800) 284-1114

Email: ctinfo@ctpub.com

Website: www.ctpub.com

C&T Publishing's professional photography services are now available to the public. Visit us at www.ctmediaservices.com.

For quilting supplies:

Cotton Patch

1025 Brown Ave.

Lafayette, CA 94549

(800) 835-4418 or

(925) 283-7883

Email: CottonPa@aol.com

Website: www.quiltusa.com

Blue Bamboo

12865 Industrial Park Blvd.

Plymouth, MN 55441

(800) 323-1105

Email: Bluebamboo@visi.com

Website: www.mybluebamboo.com

Note: Fabrics used in the quilts shown may not be currently available, as fabric manufacturers keep most fabrics in print for only a short time.

For Clearview Triangle ruler:

Alicia's Attic

204 N Link Lane #7

Fort Collins, CO 80524

(970) 224-1336

(888) 348-6653

Website: www.aliciasattic.com

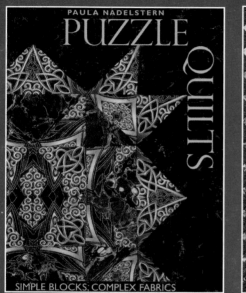
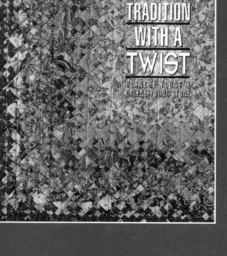
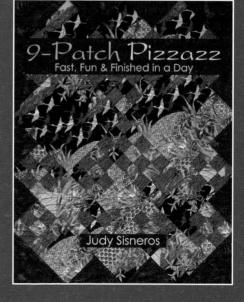